Praise for

You Make Your Path by Walking

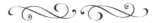

"It is our time to become living embodiments of a new human story. We must create a womb of becoming for ourselves and others beyond victimhood and being knocked down by the complexity and uncertainty of our times. What Suzanne Anderson offers in this book is a marvelous pathway to become the possible human through the challenging circumstances in our lives. Why are you here? You are here because you feel the call to step out of old ways of being and doing and not fall back to the 'same old, same old'. You are here because you feel the quickening to respond to the evolutionary instinct that demands your higher becoming. And some of you are here because you suspect that you have been called to help midwife the greatest change in human history and create a world that works for everyone. Reading this remarkable book will put you on the path of becoming all that you can and must be in these extraordinary times."

—**Jean Houston, PhD,** author of *The Possible Human,*
The Search for the Beloved and *A Passion for the Possible*

"This book has the means to touch your heart, open your mind and give you access to the journey through the eyes of a wisdom keeper. I have been so touched by Suzanne's gift of language and her wisdom of navigating the underworld. What a beautiful piece of work! Thank you for sharing your journey and allowing me to learn from you. Only a Scorpio can take you into the realms of death with such fearlessness!"

—**Debra Silverman,** astrologer and author of *The Missing Element: Inspiring Compassion for the Human Condition*

"Through the intimate revelation of her lived experience following the loss of her beloved husband to suicide, and by sharing the principles she used in coaching other women to navigate her own grief in the aftermath of unimaginable trauma, Suzanne Anderson weaves an exquisite tapestry of love, hope, and healing she invites us to apply in our own lives.

This book is a moving primer for how to "make the path by walking" we each must forge through challenging life experiences we will all encounter. With courage, grace, and wisdom, she demonstrates how, regardless of our circumstances, individually and collectively, we hold the power to heal, envision, and create a better world."
—**Donna Stoneham, PhD**, author of *Catch Me When I Fall: Poems of Mother Loss and Healing* and *The Thriver's Edge: Seven Keys to Transform the Way You Live, Love, and Lead*

"It's impossible to read this book without being profoundly moved and forever changed. Masterful. Magical. Devastatingly honest and irresistibly compelling. As Anderson guides us through her underworld, navigating the trauma of her husband's suicide, her heroine's journey becomes our own. I found myself revisiting my own traumas to experience a depth of healing that has eluded my best efforts at reconciliation for decades. This is a book that doesn't just change our lives, it can renew them."
—**Will Wilkinson**, author of *Now or Never* and co-author of *Thriving in Business and Life*

"We live in a world rife with endings. Suzanne gives us hard-won, grounded guide stones with which to navigate the territory of loss and grief. You will be reassured that down under your broken heart is a deeper humanity and profound sense of self . . . . A serious, honest, courageous book."
—**Barbara Cecil**, author of *Coming Into Your Own: A Woman's Guide Through Life Transitions*

"*You Make Your Path By Walking* offers an absorbing story of how a life changing tragedy experienced by the author sparked a life affirming journey. When her beloved husband of many years suddenly commited suicide, she had a choice. She could succumb to the dark forces unleashed by his death or confront them. She chose the latter, ultimately awakening to a higher, more expanded level of consciousness. Anderson writes a candid account of her struggles and the leviathan effort of building a new life. Throughout the process she drew upon her deep spirituality, the love of friends and the Mysterial Woman principles she taught in her professional life. The result is a poignant, instructive, and inspirational read."
—**Julie Benezet**, author of *The Journey of Not Knowing: How 21st Century Leaders Can Chart a Course Where There Is None*

You Make
Your Path
by Walking

Published 2023
Printed in the United States of America
Print ISBN: 978-1-64742-442-8
E-ISBN: 978-1-64742-443-5
Library of Congress Control Number: 2023902958

For information, address:
She Writes Press
1569 Solano Ave #546
Berkeley, CA 94707

Interior Design by Tabitha Lahr
Cover painting by Lynda Lowe

She Writes Press is a division of SparkPoint Studio, LLC.

I am deeply grateful to my sister Mysterial, Lynda Lowe, for the use of her evocative painting "Deeper Well" for the front cover. Lynda skillfully guides us between the realms of dark and light in her inspirational art, using rich archetypal and metaphorical images. This painting has a direct link to Lynda's painting "Boundless" on the cover of my first book The Way of the Mysterial Woman: Upgrading How You Live, Love and Lead *with the same beautiful vessel as the central image in both. The vessel, a Feminine container that is both empty and full with potential at the same time, invites us to drink from the deeper well as we make our paths by walking into the mystery. www.lyndalowe.com.*

You Make Your Path by Walking

A Transformational Field Guide Through Trauma and Loss

Suzanne Anderson

SHE WRITES PRESS

This book is dedicated to those brave souls who stand as shape-shifters on the frothy edge of evolution, allowing their breaking-open to be a breaking-through to a whole new level of consciousness and the capacity to positively shape the future for all beings.

Contents

PART THREE: RETURN

Introduction

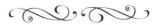

"Travelers, there is no path,
paths are made by walking."

—Antonio Machado

On January 3, 2013, my husband took his own life—and with that one devastating choice he also took my life as I knew it. This is the story of the life before that event, but mostly it is the story of what came after. It is the story of the path I walked through trauma and loss. But it is so much more than that. This is the story of a new consciousness emerging—one that we are all being called to embrace—a new way of being that is a match for the complexity and challenges of these times. It is a clarion call from our future selves, encouraging us to go into the dark when summoned by life and allow the fire of transformation to burn brightly so that we can become the ones future generations are grateful for.

There is no one single, definitive path through trauma and loss. You make your path by courageously walking one step at a time—how you journey through the shattering has everything to do with where you end up. This book is my lived experience of learning to drink from a deeper well, see in a darker night, and allow my falling apart to reveal my wholeness.

Some of you will read this when you are already tumbling down into the abyss personally—when things you thought you could count on about yourself and your life are getting pulled out to sea by some unwanted and unwelcome tidal undertow. Some of you will read this when what you've always thought was solid ground underneath you is just beginning to shake and you sense a change is on its way. Some of you will read this as you face into the darkness and uncertainty of these global times wondering how you—*we*—will survive.

However you come to this book, I hope that my own journey through loss and transformation offers you a sense of possibility and hope. Although no one wants their life to fall apart, the times we are living through are definitely requiring us to let go of old beliefs about ourselves and the world we live in.

Before the day of my husband's death I already understood something of this. I had been guiding women to move through their own suffering, confusion, anxiety, and depression and awaken to a more expanded consciousness and leadership capacity. It was very helpful for them to put their own trauma and loss inside a larger context of evolutionary unfolding; doing so allowed them to move with, rather than against, the forces of change.

I had spent twelve years researching a developmental pathway for women that would allow for all the Feminine and Masculine strengths to be developed and integrated together. I had written about this in my first book, *The Way of the Mysterial Woman: Upgrading How You Live, Love, and Lead,* coauthored with my colleague Susan Cannon.

We were witnessing profoundly new ways of living, loving, and leading consistently emerging in women willing to descend into their own depths, unhook from old shadow patterns, and liberate the next level of their potential. This remarkable ability to partner with the *Mystery*, and to express a *Medial* capacity to bridge between differences and hold a middle way through challenges, was so unprecedented that we created the word "Mysterial" to describe it. (See *The Way of the Mysterial Woman* for a more comprehensive exploration, as well as practices for cultivating each of the archetypes on the Mysterial pathway.)

In the course of our working and writing together, Susan and I began to identify eight unprecedented strengths that were emerging in the women who had completed our programs, what we called "Mysterial Meta-Capacities." These were exactly the strengths that I would draw on in the aftermath of David's suicide and the unraveling of my life.

In part one of this book I will take you into my life before, during and after the shocking event of my husband's suicide and the dismantling of my life; in part two I will take you deeply into each of the eight critical capacities that helped me meet my shattered inner and outer worlds and rebuild a robust new life; and in part three I will offer some of the inner tools, rituals, and broader perspectives needed to transform through trauma and loss.

The chaos, disruption, and dismantling of my old life, while incredibly difficult, also created the conditions for me to grow and develop in powerful ways. I believe that we need to cultivate the next level of our emotional, social, and mental capacities to meet the challenges not only of our personal lives, but also of an increasingly complex, interconnected, and uncertain world. To paraphrase Einstein, we can't solve the problems of today with the consciousness that created them yesterday. The good news is that we have an evolutionary tailwind that can push us forward in our development—*if* we can just stop resisting this tailwind, both in our personal lives and our collective experience, and welcome in the forces of transformation.

In these unraveling times there will be the breaking down and the breaking apart of many things that we have held as precious: our identity, our way of life, our relationships . . . all these things that we cling to and don't want to change. The light of our former lives may flicker and sometimes, as in my case, go out completely.

Yet something that I might now call the *hidden wholeness* is present in the darkness that ensues. It has always been there. It was there, quietly waiting for me, at the threshold between my old life and the one that was yet to emerge. In the days that followed my husband's chosen death and the loss of everything that mattered most to me, this sense of faith in something that could not be broken did not abandon me. It was simply there. And the Mysterial Meta-Capacities were like the guiding breadcrumbs that led me through the dark forest and into this place of Presence.

This deeper call to wholeness is whispering to us all. Do you hear it in your life?

For me the call came just when I thought everything was coming into place in my life.

My coauthor and I were ready to stride into the world with our book and a new program to bring this message and pathway for a quantum leap in women's growth. The timing seemed perfect. But that was before Life said, "Not so fast, Suzanne. How do you know if this new Mysterial way of being will hold up even when *everything* falls apart? How will you manage when all that matters most to you is ripped away and you are left alone on the barren shore of a new life? Will you use the fire of trauma to transform? Will you live as a Mysterial then?"

In my experience, the liberation of the next level of our potential—the new gene code that is a match for these times—can be accelerated through the fire of trauma and loss. This is not the only way that development can occur, but when personal or collective crises happen, we can harness the energy for transformation. I did not know this when my life was dismantled overnight—but I do now, and it makes sense. In a thriving forest, the seeds for future growth are released when a fire burns through, seemingly leaving only smoking embers and black ash behind. Likewise, the seeds of our Mysterial potential can be activated in the searing heat of trauma and loss.

This is the story of my journey and how I made my path through traumatic loss and into transformation by walking the Mysterial way and cultivating the deeper root system of the Meta-Capacities—a system that I had only glimpsed the seed potential of before.

I want this book to be an encouragement for you to make your own path by walking across the hot coals of loss toward, not away from, fear and uncertainty. I want it to be a true tone ringing in the discomfort of darkness, like a singing bowl signaling that these times are a threshold crossing ushering you into a new world.

I will share with you how I did that—how I found my way to embody resilience, surrender to the Great Mystery, and find my way home to a deeper sense of myself.

Although this is a story about my past, it is also a guide for our present and a talisman of hope for the future that can inspire us to keep walking even when we are sure we cannot.

Part One:

Origin

A MYTHIC JOURNEY

Part I

Myths have been guiding narratives for me for many years. Collective myths are like the DNA of the human psyche, providing the codes that shape perception, understanding, and behaviors. In my first book, *The Way of the Mysterial Woman*, we used the Greek Persephone/Demeter myth as a heroine's journey guiding map for women. Like the Sumerian Inanna and the Egyptian Isis myths, the basic plotline is descent, dismantling, transformation, and rebirth.

One day as I looked back over the fragments of these past years since David's death, I realized that I had been on my own variation of this mythic journey. It was powerful for me to frame my personal story as a mythic, archetypal, and collective story of loss and transformation.

I will share the beginning of my myth here, and throughout the book I will offer you the remaining fragments of my odyssey through the darkness, written in mythic terms. If you are going through a difficult descent, there may come a moment when you too are able to lift your eyes off of the trail in front of you and let the narrative thread of your own journey be seen in a larger mythic arc.

Once upon a time there was a charismatic king who lived in a beautiful castle on a peaceful island. But this had not always been so. For many years he'd wandered the world, a would-be king who lived between the realms in search of his kingdom.

One day the fates guided him to a Pacific Northwest island and a rare piece of land looking out over the sea. He walked upon the mosses beneath the towering cedars swaying in the wind, heard the ravens call three times, and made his way to the top of the hill—where he found, stretched out before him across the sea, the majestic, snow-capped Olympic mountains. He fell to his knees and wept, for he knew that he had finally found home. This was the place where he would build the otherworldly sanctuary that he had seen in a vision many years before.

Traveling the world, he found ancient buildings in faraway lands and brought them to his sanctuary—rebuilding them piece by piece. He gathered centuries-old steppingstones, rare vessels, and antique furniture, shaping his kingdom into a place like no other.

Over many years he poured all his resources into this masterpiece, and he was proud of his creation. But he was also lonely. A kingdom without anyone in it can be a hollow home. Yet he never imagined that he could find someone of this world who could light his heart afire as much as the beautiful place he'd created and his divine friends in other realms.

While the king sat alone in his castle, not far away, in a cottage at the water's edge, was a wise healer woman who was also making her way alone in the world.

One day the fates brought them together. They fit into each other like puzzle pieces just waiting to be matched, filling in the places in one another that they hadn't even known were empty. Love grew quickly, and before long she became his queen.

Chapter 1:

Encountering My Beloved

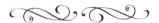

*"The minute I heard my first love story,
I started looking for you, not knowing how
blind that was. Lovers don't finally meet
somewhere, they're in each other all along."*

—Rumi

Rumi says that when you meet your beloved you see that they have been in you all along. That's how I felt when I met David—that I'd been moving toward him my whole life. I was coded from as far back as I can remember to fall in love with a "David," and I can see now that every step of my life was taking me toward him.

When I was old enough to have crushes on boys, somehow the idea was already in my head that my true love was named David. I don't know where that idea came from—perhaps something I saw on TV, a character in a book I read, or my destiny. I just knew.

Throughout my twenties and thirties, whenever I met a man named David, I would wonder if he was the one. It was a crazy game I played with myself, trying to figure out if this was *the* David fate had in mind for me. Eventually I fell in love with someone named

Robert and I remember being surprised, but when I met his father and discovered that *his* name was David, I thought that was close enough.

My relationship with Robert was passionate and tumultuous from the very beginning. We met in Canada while we were both on a one week cleansing program friends of mine were running in a remote cottage on a lake north of Toronto. I remember that when they told me the list of who was coming to the retreat, a quiet ping of recognition went off inside me as they said his name. I would often get these sonar hits when someone or some place that was going to be important to me was named.

Robert was exiting a failing marriage and launching a medical device company in southern France. I was single and jet-setting between Toronto and Paris as an international leadership consultant. I already knew that some big changes were coming in my life.

A few months after I met Robert, when I was burning out from my demanding consulting practice and was in search of answers and my own healing, I took a trip to Bali, Indonesia, to visit my sister, Hannah. As we traveled around that beautiful green jewel, I began to drop into the exhaustion in my body that I had been too numb before to feel. My senses drank in the sweet smells of early-morning jasmine, the evocative sounds of chanting, the sights of women with prayer baskets balanced carefully on their heads, and the feeling of the warm, humid air on my bare skin. As we fasted, meditated, and took long walks on the beach, something started to shift inside of me.

Early one morning, sitting above the layered rice fields, I was carried into an altered state. It was as though my ego just fell away and the distinctions of identity melted away, leaving me in a blissful union with everything.

While in this state a deep inquiry came into my awareness, not as a question to be answered but more as an invitation to be received: *Will you help to midwife the Divine Feminine on earth?*

There was no mind engaged trying to come up with an answer—that capacity was offline. But every cell in my body unequivocally responded *yes*.

When, after forty-eight hours, I came out of this soft, expansive, loving state, my personality began to reorganize itself again. I remembered the question and that I had said yes to it. But I had no idea what that meant. Up until then my own spiritual path had been more centered around a masculine spiritual teacher, and I had very little understanding of what the Divine Feminine actually was.

Many years later, I would come to understand the energy that suffused my being as akin to the archetype of Kuan Yin, the Goddess of Compassion. In the meantime, my relationship with Robert seemed an important part of my *yes*, and I trusted it would carry me into my new life.

Our love affair took off quickly and was full of excitement and magic as we met in Paris and other exotic locations. We both felt that fate had called us together and would carry us into some new and hopeful world.

During one of our holidays in Crete, we were both awakened out of our dreams at the same time. It was the middle of the night and our little stone cottage high up in the hills was enveloped in total darkness and silence. When I realized Robert was awake too, I turned toward him and said, "I have just had the most amazing dream."

"Me too!" he replied with a smile.

"A beautiful young girl with curly, blond, Shirley Temple–like hair came to me and said she wanted to be my child," I told him. "In the dream it was like I knew her already and was so happy to see her again. And I told her that of course I would be her mother."

Robert stammered out, "I saw the same little girl in my dream!"

We were already people who watched for synchronous signs and signals, and this seemed to confirm that we should get married and have this baby girl together.

Within two years we were indeed married.

But in order to fulfill the other promise of the dream, my forty-plus-year-old body required many interventions, escalating from fertility drugs, to artificial insemination, to in vitro fertilization, and finally to a simple surgical procedure to unblock my fallopian tubes. Once that was done, I got pregnant quickly—but apparently my eggs weren't a match for my enthusiasm. After four pregnancies and four miscarriages over the course of four years, I somehow still found the strength to keep moving forward.

Through the intensity of this process, Robert and I fused together more and more in our hope and grief. There was little breathing room in our relationship and my creative autonomy was slowly being snuffed out. My previously expansive world began to shrink, smaller and smaller, until there was little left in it but Robert and our crashing dreams of having a child.

And then everything changed.

On September 11th, 2001 when a tremor of violent terrorism shook all of us in the western world, something woke up inside of me. The invitation that I had accepted years before in Bali to help "midwife the Divine Feminine on earth" snapped back into clear focus. I could not imagine directing my energy toward one child, when I sensed I would be needed to guide many women into the consciousness and leadership capacity to steer us through the rocky time ahead.

Suddenly, everything I had begun to orient my life around—my marriage, our home, having a child—no longer felt correct. It was not a mental decision so much as it was an embodied knowing that my true calling was the work I was beginning to do with women. And fulfilling that purpose would require sacrifice.

In the years since that moment, I have come to know and teach that when our nos arise in response to our deepest yeses in life, there is a solid ground on which we can stand and bear what must be lost. We have often been taught to make our decisions through our linear left brain alone and to distrust our emotional or bodily knowing. This is one of the ways that we have internalized the patriarchy.

Often we don't want to know what we know because then we would have to do something about it. And we don't want to rock the boat or be rejected. So we use different techniques, depending on our personality's ego defenses, to not know.

For some it might be numbing out with TV, addictive substances, overworking, overextending to take care of others, keeping occupied with continuous improvement of something that just isn't ready for prime time, overdramatizing the moment so that emotional chaos keeps you from knowing, staying in your head with constant analysis, or using self-doubt to keep you from your truth.

For me it was about pouring myself into the baby-making project and rationalizing that I couldn't fully follow my first calling while also responding to my second calling to have this baby girl. Instead of honoring my deep, intuitive calling to help birth the Divine Feminine, which might disrupt my marriage and our hopes for a child, I let myself become a little lost inside my very contracted world and allowed my inner dream to fade away as I created more space for a baby.

As if to test my newfound resolve to reorient the focus of my life, four days after the shock and horror of 9/11 I got a call from the Reproductive Care at UW Medical Center telling me that after eighteen months my name had finally come to the top of the egg donor list. Healthy, young eggs were available for us to scramble together with Robert's sperm and hopefully serve up as a baby. I had forgotten I had even put my name on this list.

When the call came from the clinic, I received the news with uncertainty rather than excitement. The terrorist attacks had reawakened my deeper calling, and now this bridge that was being offered to me into the land of motherhood seemed wrong. My colleague Susan and I had just begun teaching our Women's Integral Leadership Programs through Antioch University in Seattle and we were starting to get traction.

I asked for a few days to think it over, but I already felt sure that I was not going to go through this stressful and time-consuming process of getting pregnant. I simply knew that my destiny was no longer aligned with the probability path of having a child.

I also knew that my decision to not move forward with trying to have a baby would rock the already shaky foundation of my relationship with Robert.

Although it took several months for our marriage to grind to its very painful halt, the course was set on that day when the *no* took shape inside me. Robert wanted a family more than anything else—and he did go on to remarry and have three beautiful boys. I, meanwhile, committed myself to becoming a Divine Feminine changemaker in these tipping-point times and stepped forward into that mystery.

———

In the rough waters of the dissolution of my marriage, I could never have imagined that my *yes* to diving full on into my work with women was also the tributary that would lead me to *my* David.

By November Robert had found an apartment in Seattle, moved out, and thrust us into the painful process of divorce. He felt betrayed by me and I felt betrayed by him. We were both angry, bitter, and very sad.

I felt like a failure at every level. As a member of a family that had never had anyone divorce before, the shame of my divorce hung over me like a dark cloud. And the failure to become a mother and have children left me with an empty womb. I was being ripped farther and farther away from the familiar landmarks of domestic womanhood—husband, children, home—and into the strange new landscape of being a barren soon-to-be divorcee renting a house and launching a women's leadership business.

By April we had finally agreed to the terms of mediation. After a visit with my lawyer that month, it suddenly struck me that I was going to get divorced. Having dinner with some girlfriends later that night, I turned the word over and over again in my mouth, practicing saying, "I am getting divorced, I am a divorc-ee." It felt refreshing to say it out loud, to acknowledge the unlikely "divorced" shore that I had suddenly washed up on.

It was late when I left the restaurant and sped across the West Seattle bridge hoping to catch the last ferry back to my home on

Vashon Island. Directly ahead of me was a gray Saab that was also going above the speed limit and was maneuvering around traffic and through yellow lights in a way that I recognized as a fellow ferry commuter. I was in luck.

Best-case scenario when going over the speed limit to get to the Fauntleroy ferry dock is to find another car ahead who is doing the same and get in their slipstream. It is a bit like being a biker in a fast-moving peloton drafting behind the leader: a nice, safe spot to be if there happens to be a police car in the area.

I liked how the driver held the road and drove with speed and confidence. It reminded me of driving in France and how I missed that boldness in the politically correct, slow-driving Pacific Northwest. I had often been stuck behind "dinkers," as I lovingly called them, when I was trying to make a ferry, and there was nothing more frustrating.

"If I make this ferry I am going to thank the driver of that car," I said to myself. "They are really driving!"

The gray Saab flew onto the boat and me right after it, the last car before the ferry pulled away from the dock. I was still clutching the steering wheel, adrenaline rushing through my body, when the driver of the car walked past me on his way to the upper deck. I recognized him as a man whom I had first seen walking down Burma Road by my house, sporting an oversize green corduroy coat, short baggy pants, and a green beanie cap. I'd thought he was the homeless man living in the woods near my house that I had heard about until I had seen him at an Indian music and dance performance at his home a few months before. This was David Smith.

I couldn't believe the synchronicity. About six months earlier, just after I had told Robert I no longer wanted to pursue trying to have a baby together, I'd learned there was a concert in a Balinese temple just up the road. As soon as I heard about the concert, that familiar sonar ping went off inside. Something was waiting for me there.

The evening of the Balinese concert I had walked up the hill from our Vashon home on the waterfront to the place where I was told the performance would take place. It was to be in an Indonesian temple that someone had on their property.

It was a beautiful evening, and as I walked down the winding driveway I felt excited and nervous to be entering into this new world and reconnecting with my soulful memories of Bali.

There before me appeared the most extraordinary carved teak traditional Indonesian temple, with a large, swooping roof and a carved inner Joglo. Everything oozed with the folk magic of Java. The place was buzzing—people gathering, musicians rushing about trying to get the sound system to work. I remember scanning the others, all the cool-looking men and women present, and wondering what had happened to my life. I used to know people like this; before my life shrank into a thimble that held only my marriage with Robert and our miscarriages, I had once had a dynamic life.

I turned to the person next to me and asked, "Who lives in this place, and what is the story behind it?"

"See the man over there helping with the lights?" She gestured in his direction. "It's his place. That's David Smith, the owner of David Smith & Co—you know, the furniture store that sells all those amazing furniture pieces and artwork from Indonesia?"

I did know that store; I drove past it often, and had even taken my sister, Hannah, and her husband in there when they were visiting. Entering the store was like entering another world, so it made sense that his home also felt otherworldly.

"He lives in a house over there," she continued, pointing up the hill behind the building.

"He lives there by himself. I think maybe he's gay."

As soon as she said the name David, I felt a jolt inside. I looked over at the elegant man she had pointed to and felt an immediate sense of recognition. He had on white pants and a white sweatshirt, and had an eccentric English look about him that I found very attractive. He was barefoot, with long legs and arms and a broad smile that he flashed around generously to everyone in his vicinity.

So yes, I knew who this man was that I had followed onto the ferry, and as he walked by my car I zipped down my window and said, chuckling, "I love the way you drive. You went through some yellow lights."

"Well, you went through some red lights!" he responded, laughing, his eyes twinkling.

We were both a bit giddy from our high-speed escapade through West Seattle—like we'd gotten away with something we shouldn't have.

"You coming up?" he asked, pointing to the upstairs of the ferry.

I nodded. "Sounds good."

I climbed out of my car and followed him to the upper deck—which, at that late hour, was mostly empty—delighted to have company for the twenty-minute ride home. I was feeling the buzz from the wine I'd had with my girlfriends, the anxiety of my new identity as an almost newly minted divorcee, and the rush of the drive. It was all rather intoxicating. Good thing I was talking to a *gay guy*.

People always loved this next part of the story of how we met. We each told it very differently.

My version: I was happy to be on the ferry and talking to a safe gay man about the new reality of getting a divorce. What it meant for me to be the first one in my family to divorce. How angry my husband was and how I had hired a very strong lawyer to help me stand firmly on my own ground and get what was rightly mine.

David's version: Suzanne said the word *divorced* at least ten times. It was clear that she was wanting me to know that she was available. She was coming on to me and I was fine with that.

Before we left to go back to our cars I told David that I was selling the waterfront home Robert and I had shared. He said that he would like to come and see it, so of course I gave him my number. I found him handsome and charming—too bad he was gay.

A few days later, David came to my house with his best friend, Phil, ostensibly to take a look before I put it on the market. I had not yet seen his full estate, so I didn't know just how ridiculous it would be for him to be interested in buying my house.

I toured them around my home and I did find it a bit odd that David seemed to be more interested in the books on my bookshelf, in the fact that I read *The New York Times*, and in speaking about

various artifacts I had from Indonesia, than he was in actually looking at the house.

I learned later that when he drove out of my driveway he turned
to Phil and said, "Now why can't I find a woman like that?"

To which Phil responded, "Because, Dave, you only date women
half your age!"

A few days later, David called and asked, "Would you like to have
tea at my teahouse just down the beach from you on Sunday afternoon?"

It sounded charming. I was delighted at the potential of making
a new friend amidst so much change in my life.

The tide was low enough that I could walk the short distance down
the beach from my home to the little boathouse on stilts that David
had transformed into a Thoreau-on-Walden-Pond kind of place.
Along with his larger home up the hill from me, he had created this
magical refuge in an unused boathouse. He had spotted it one day
while walking on the beach and in typical David fashion, before the
week was out, he had made an arrangement with the owner to use
the boathouse in exchange for creating an antique stone pathway
to her house. He'd had special windows and skylights made in
his workshop in Java for his teahouse, and the afternoon sunlight
poured in through them as the high tide swooshed back and forth
under the floorboards, creating a soothing, rhythmic sound.

In the corner of the room was a small, round, three-legged table,
upon which was a simple brown oolong teapot from China and a
candle. An Indonesian daybed with an indigo blue cover from Bali
was the place for napping—or, I imagined reading poetry—in the
languorous afternoons. There were a few antique chairs scattered
around, and an old sheepskin was tucked under the table. It was the
place where, I would learn, David felt most at home—the place in
right proportion to his being.

I was spellbound from the moment I entered, and my own inner
poetic muse, which had been dormant for the many months of my
tumultuous divorce process, woke wide up.

The difference between our two worlds was never as apparent as it was at that first tea together. I was a tea snob and had brought an exquisite black tea blend called Opera that I had shipped in directly from Paris every three months. I had also brought my freshly baked scones, which were my specialty.

David, it turned out, was also a tea snob, but his specialty was the green end of the spectrum. And his snack was a gelatinous Japanese mochi.

No, he would not have my black tea with milk, as he was lactose intolerant and the caffeine of the black tea would be too much. And no, he could not eat my scones, because he was gluten intolerant.

And so I put down my little basket of goodies and crossed over into his world.

The green tea was delicious and the mochi an adventure. When I close my eyes I can still smell the aroma of the old wood, green tea, and briny seashore mixing together into a scent that felt like home.

In some ways I think David was never happier than when he was in that small boathouse, a place cozy and uncomplicated in its simplicity.

I think it took him back to a simpler time in his life, when he was just starting out. From his early roots teaching yoga in Seattle he found his way to Esalen in Big Sur California, a retreat center at the heart of the human potential movement in the 1970s. It was there that he met a friend who inspired him to go to Indonesia and experience the spiritual beauty of Bali.

He wrote these words about his experience of arriving there: "Everything shimmered with an emerald dizziness, then the distant silhouette of three volcanoes grasped hold and rooted me in place, and everything assembled into this: a hilly middle distance bursting with the green exuberance of coconut fronds, while directly before me farmers in their bamboo sun hats shuttled back and forth, yoked to their oxen on the steep slopes that had been carved into farm plots down to the river."

He was smitten. It wasn't long before he was inspired by the elaborate bead patterns on the back of the cloth baby carriers that women used in Borneo and decided to have beads sewn directly onto the back of denim jackets to mimic this beauty. He would have these made in Bali and sell them in the US. He had stumbled into a career perfectly suited to his free-spirited nature, and it gave him his first taste of unbounded creativity.

Later on, as he drove his motorbike around Bali, he began to notice antique shops selling furniture from Java popping up like mushrooms after the rain. He had stumbled upon the beginnings of a diaspora of teak—quirky village furniture that had sat in place for 100 years in Java. Antique collectors were buying these unique pieces from the original family owners and selling them to an increasing number of foreign dealers who loaded the precious furniture into containers and sent them all over the world. He became one of these antique hunters, and thus began his iconic teak furniture business in Seattle. It grew from a small warehouse down by the shipping docks to David Smith & Co, a 14,000-square-foot brick building in South Lake Union.

He found the property on Vashon Island when he was looking for a location to put a rare teak building from Kudus in eastern Java that he had bought. He had disassembled and moved it to his Javanese workshop, numbering all the pieces so that it was like a giant LEGO kit, and was determined to bring it to the United States. When he found the land on Vashon, he built himself a home and then shipped multiple containers full of his Kudus teak building components and brought over two Javanese carpenters to put it back together again. Soon, the temple-like structure rose up on the land—and that, it turned out, was just the beginning. In the years to come, he would bring over a number of other buildings, creating an otherworldly domain with exotic architecture, stones from China, Japanese rock gardens, and natural beauty carefully placed throughout its seventeen acres. This property, the buildings, and the gardens on it would become his central passion and the canvas for his remarkable expression of soulful beauty.

It was into this magical world that I was drawn. Many months passed with us meeting now and again for tea and long conversations at his house, at mine, and in the boathouse. I loved our times together, and I felt like I was building a new and important friendship with someone who wasn't interested in women.

One day as I was talking to my hair stylist, whom I had seen ever since I moved to Seattle, he said, "You have a little sparkle in your eyes today . . . have you met someone new?"

"Well I do have a new friend whom I am attracted to, but I think he is gay," I offered.

My stylist, who was himself gay, declared that he had good "gaydar" and, arching an eyebrow, asked me to tell him more about this gentleman.

"Well, there was something odd that happened this weekend when we were having tea at his boathouse," I said. "He told me that he had just had a conversation with his mother, with whom he's very close, in which he'd asked her, 'Do you think I will ever get married, Mom?' And she responded with, 'Well, Dave, maybe someday.'"

"Is there any spark or chemistry between you?" my stylist broke in.

"Yes, I think so—at least I certainly feel it, and I think he does too."

"Well then," he proclaimed, "he is not gay. If there was chemistry and he was gay, he would have said something like, 'And my mother said no, Dave, you're gay and marriage isn't legal yet.' He would have wanted you to know that he wasn't available."

That perspective suddenly opened up a whole new world for me. Now there was a little more energy in me when I was around David, and I also allowed myself to flirt.

One day, not long after my illuminating conversation at the hair salon, I invited David over to my house for tea. We were immersed in one of our captivating conversations when I heard a startling thunk against my living room window. I knew immediately it was the sound of a bird accidentally slamming into the huge picture window. Without explaining myself, I leapt up from my seat and ran outside to check on the bird. I gathered the wounded sparrow into my hands and held it, sending soothing energy into the little bird. I noticed David watching me silently with a curious expression on his face.

Once the bird had recovered from being stunned, it fluttered from my hands and soared back into the sky. We went inside and resumed our conversation and tea. David would later tell me that when I held the injured bird in my cupped palms it reminded him of a time when he was a child and held an injured bird in his hands. In that instant, he said, something inside him awakened to the possibility of loving me and being loved by me, like an unknown inner door had been unlocked by the right key and suddenly swung open.

About a week later—not surprisingly, in his little boathouse where we first had tea together—we crossed over the threshold into intimacy. It was a sunny June afternoon, and after our cup of green tea and mochi and conversations about the universe, David invited me onto his antique daybed for a little afternoon nap. When his warm lips touched mine, I felt like our destiny lines—lines that had been arcing toward each other all our lives, and maybe even for multiple lifetimes—finally came together. A current of energy moved through me that I had never felt before and I settled into his arms. It felt like some burden I had been carrying all my life had just dropped away. I felt safe and at home.

⸺

And so it began—ten years with *my* David, who had been in me all along. When eventually I moved in with him, his house came alive. Prior to my living there, it had been like an antique furniture sales room with nothing but hard teak furniture and Chinese chairs. I brought soft sofas, colorful cushions, lamps, dinner parties with friends, golden lighting, and the hum of coziness. And just as I brought David and his house alive, his loving and steady presence healed a lifelong loneliness in me and filled me with a deep sense of belonging. We both awakened to what it was to truly care for and be cared for by another person as we discovered the profound healing that can come through unconditional love.

Our favorite times were at home. Sunday mornings, with music playing, we would tuck ourselves into the corner table in the kitchen with the Sunday *New York Times*. I would begin with the Week in Review and Sunday Styles and he would read the Front Page section and flip through the Sunday magazine, ripping out images of beautiful designer furniture or decorations that caught his eye. My cat, Emma, would curl up beside us, purring her contentment.

I was home. I remember early on in our relationship sitting next to David in the Indonesian Kudus temple building listening to Shujaat Khan, a world-famous sitar musician, playing a riff with the tabla player, and feeling all the cells of my body streaming into some new formation. I was perched on my cushion up at the front of the room, nestled in next to my beloved, feeling like a queen beside her king. I belonged. To him. To this place. To life.

⌣

Our wedding was a memorable day of love, beauty, poetry, and magic. In my work with women, I had guided them through the journey required for a sacred inner marriage which culminated in a potent wedding ceremony of Feminine and Masculine Union. It was a profound fulfillment for me to experience this with David in the outer world.

For several days before the wedding, I could feel the forces of the Divine Feminine flowing powerfully through my body. It took a lot for me to stay grounded with this energy moving, and I gave it lots of spacious room inside myself. On the day of the wedding, I began to shift my awareness from all the wedding details to becoming the archetypal bride ready to meet her beloved at the altar.

All the guests were invited to gather in the Kudus temple building, and as they took their places musicians Jessika and Ervind brought the words of the Persian poet Hafiz to life in an ethereal ballad. Up at the house I could hear the strains of the ancient music and knew it was time for me to go to David. My wedding party gathered, with my nieces up front as the Maidens, two women with me as the Mothers, and two dear friends behind holding the energy of the Crone. With our parasols up, we walked slowly and deliberately down the stone path toward the Kudus House.

David and Eshin, the Buddhist priest who would conduct our ceremony, took their places inside the building. I circumambulated the Kudus temple, allowing the energy of the Divine Feminine to come fully into my body. When I turned the final corner, put down my parasol, and stepped through the carved doorway, I was swept into another realm. My beloved reached out his hands and drew me in beside him.

A Mythic Journey

Part II

The king and queen lived happily together for the next countless moons. Many people in the realm were drawn to visit their castle, and where there once was only silence there was now joy, love, music, dance, song, and prayer. The healing beauty of the place was known throughout the land.

And so it continued, until a profound disquiet began to gnaw at the king's heart and his head began to screech with a strange sound. He had built his castle in the air, held together by gossamer dreams, and it was all beginning to crumble down around him now. He did not have the courage to tell his queen the truth about the disappearing world, and he did not have the strength to rebuild everything. For so many years he had been a great alchemist, turning lead into gold— but it had come at a cost and now, with the noise inside his head, he could not enter into the realms of magic. He was left with only his earthly world, and that was falling apart.

Although he tried hard to hide his doubts and fears, his queen sensed that all was not well with her king. She searched the land for healing salves for the thundering noise building inside his head. She sang him songs and showed him images of a future when he would again find peace. But she did not see the devastating earthquake coming that would shake them both right out of the kingdom.

Chapter 2:

The Ground Begins to Crumble

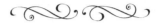

"When your eyes are tired
the world is tired also.
When your vision has gone
no part of the world can find you."

—DAVID WHYTE

When David turned into his sixth decade on October 20, 2012, I threw a big party with his family and all of his closest friends. It was a real threshold crossing for him, as he'd never imagined he would live until sixty. He told me that he'd had a nagging feeling throughout his life that he wasn't going to be long on this earth.

Even though he had resisted my plans for this party, when the night finally came he was deeply happy to have his dearest friends and family there with him. The house was full of laughter and joy— candles glowing everywhere, fire crackling in the fireplace, music rocking through our great sound system, and catered Indonesian finger food scattered about. It was the perfect party.

To start the night off I made a toast to him. Standing in front of the fireplace, completely relaxed in the role of MC in front of all these people I knew and loved so well, I spoke about how I once thought David, with his eclectic clothes and wandering ways, was homeless, and how I would send him compassion and blessings every time I saw him.

"Of course when we finally met I discovered that he was anything but homeless," I said, gesturing toward the legendary island sanctuary surrounding us.

A ripple of laughter moved through the room as I continued.

I told everyone that meeting David and becoming his life partner was the best thing that had happened to me in my life. "There are many things that I love about David and the ways that he inspires me," I continued, "but the latest is something that started in May, when he returned from Bali. He came down from meditating one morning and said, 'I am having the best day of my life.' And I thought, *Great . . . wonderful*. Then the next day he did the same . . . and then two days after that the same . . . and finally after about a month of this, I said, 'You can't keep saying this anymore—how can every day be the best day of your life?'

I couldn't help but break into a huge grin as I looked out at everyone in the room and explained what he had said next. "'But it's true' he said. 'This really is—it is quantum each day. I wish you could just be me for a day.' And this morning, sure enough, he came down and said, 'I am having the best day of my life.' And I just smiled and said, 'WOW.'"

"Most of you here have known David far longer than I have," I continued, "and through many different chapters of his life. Hopefully we will hear some of those stories tonight. You know how artists have different periods—the blue period, the black period, the rose period. In the book that David is just finishing, he writes about a complex theory of awakening with three phases. You will have to buy the book to find out more about this. But here is a sneak preview of the phases: BE HERE HOW . . . BE HERE NOW . . . and BE HERE WOW."

I looked around the room, smiling. "Well I think the first phase of his life was about figuring out BE HERE HOW. The decade I have known him has been BE HERE NOW—really landing here in this place, in his life; actually having Sunday breakfast together with the New York Times—but from this day on he is heading into his BE HERE WOW period!" I raised my glass. "A toast to David Smith and his BE HERE WOW period!"

In many ways, this toast was prescient. It would only be a few short months later that all of us in the room would be living in the devastation of his WOW phase.

Not long after that celebration, as we moved through the last few months of 2012, the wheels started to come off the cart, although I did not put all these pieces together until much later.

The obvious problems began when seemingly out of nowhere David started having tinnitus. It was a kind of torture for him—an endless, loud screeching inside his head that kept him from finding the inner sanctuary where he could metabolize all the stress of his life. He was not sleeping well, and morning meditation was made impossible. He stopped exclaiming that every day was the best day of his life.

As David's stress and discomfort escalated, I was consumed with completing my Mysterial Woman book and enrolling our first public women's leadership program in over a year, which was due to launch on January 9. There was a lot to prepare, and my body was stressed. I had a daily practice of writing in a WeMoon Calendar Journal, and during this time I kept reporting that I had a throat lump or a headache.

All the while, I just assumed that David and I would make our way through whatever difficulties arose together. And even though I knew that there was no cure for tinnitus, I believed that David could overcome this—that we could overcome it together.

As we approached the winter solstice, David's suffering was coming to a peak. The solstice and equinox times had been for years a sort of ritual anchor for me, connected as they were to the Persephone/Demeter story that is a guiding myth in my women's leadership programs. December 21, 2012 was particularly significant because it was supposedly the end of the Mayan calendar and there were doomsday predictions that the world would tilt on its axis and end.

While this did not prove to be true for the planet, it did certainly portend the end of my life as I knew it.

———

For the solstice, my new friend and neighbor Antonia and I decided to participate together in an event to be hosted by a ritual elder and friend, Michael Meade, on our island. I had just run into Michael a day earlier in Thriftway, the island's main grocery store, as he was preparing to go to the local high school to speak to the students about a recent suicide. We'd commiserated about the rise in suicide among kids these days.

Antonia and I went over to the event space that morning to set up an amazing altar honoring the sun and the moon. We laid out multiple cloths and set up a lichen-covered branch where people would hang prayers they had written. There were candles everywhere, shining crystals, stones, and statues of goddesses.

I was the archetypal Sun and Antonia the archetypal Moon. Both of us theatrical in nature, we were thrilled to dress up in the archetypal energies we were portraying. I painted my face with gold sparkles, glued on long gold eyelashes, and wore elbow-length gold gloves. I wrapped myself in a golden shawl and diaphanous dress and wore a red crown from India that sparkled with fake gems. As the moon, Antonia was a glitter of silver sparkles, her crown shimmering in layers of purple and orange. She wore a silver-white shawl and moonbeam-like dress.

As we excitedly got dressed at my house, David sat alone in the living room on the sofa. When we came in to show him our costumes he was hunched over in despair, his head in his hands. It was heartbreaking to see. How had he gone, in only a few short months, from the dazzling man speaking on his sixtieth birthday with such delight about all that lay ahead to this despondent, anguished shell of a man?

Antonia and I sat with him on the sofa in our bejeweled costumes . . . Sun and Moon on either side . . . and he burst into tears.

"My head is ringing," he said. "I've finished my book and I'm scared. I feel lost and confused."

I believe that he already knew he was leaving then and was feeling the anguish of this choice, encountering our enthusiasm to embrace life even as he had lost faith in his own ability to be in his.

We encouraged him to join us at the event, and he said that he would think about it. It was hard to leave him in that moment, but we had to go to set up our altar and ignite the forces of Sun and Moon for the big community event.

Later that night, in the midst of the ritual, there was a powerful moment when we dimmed the lights and Michael, standing above the altar Antonia and I had created, read the names of all the people who had died on the island that year, some of them from suicide, as well as the names of the twenty-six children who had lost their lives in the Sandy Hook Elementary School shooting, which had happened just a few months earlier. David arrived just as this ritual was starting—eerie timing, given what was coming in a few short weeks.

I was so happy that he had come, and a great weight lifted from my shoulders as he nestled in beside me in the dark. We stood together at the altar, tenderly holding hands and listening to the names of the dead as they were read out.

In the end, he stayed only for this—and then, just as quickly as he had come, he left. The outer and inner noise was too much, he said.

The next few weeks before the end of the year were a blur. I was busy working nonstop to launch my leadership program. At the same time we were both preparing for a special wedding on January 5, when David's beloved niece Claire would be marrying David's store manager, Chris. I was excited to be a part of this love match that had been developing for a several years—a union that David took great pride in having facilitated.

Although there were invitations to join others for New Year's Eve, we decided to stay home and be quiet. I helped David compile the manuscript of his book, *Secrets of a Self-Cleaning Mind*, which he had been working on for over a year. He had chapters about his theory of awakening and chapters that told his personal stories. We put them all together into a PDF and blessed it that night. Later I would understand why he was so obsessed with writing this book and completing it by the end of the year.

We sat in front of the fireplace in our leather chairs sharing our harvest of the past year and our dreams for the year ahead.

With a cracking voice, David said, "I think I have broken something inside. I don't know what I have done—maybe it is from meditation. Or maybe I have just gone too far with things. I feel broken. I don't know if I can live like this." A tear rolled down his cheek.

I thought he was speaking about his tinnitus—that he thought the intense meditations he had experienced might have somehow activated this ringing in his ears.

I reached out and held him in my arms. "We will figure this out," I said through my own tears. "You are not broken. I am going to help you. This is life. There are hard times and easier times. You will become stronger through this suffering. Don't give up."

Years before, he had told me briefly about a period in his life when he had wanted to kill himself, but it had been a well-rounded narrative about the past, not something I could imagine the David I knew now actually doing. Later, after he died, I would read a chapter in his book that would introduce me more fully to that version of him—the one who could consider suicide.

On this New Year's Eve, some naïve part of me thought that my words encouraging him to find the strength to carry on would make all the difference and turn him back toward life. Indeed, that night they seemed to. He settled down and we were as one person sitting in front of the fire, our love for one another wrapping us both in its arms.

As the evening closed, I was hopeful. Before bed that night, I wrote in my WeMoon Journal, *Really the best New Year's—just really loving with David and me fully present, good food and then a movie. Then I massaged David—hopefully he will sleep well tonight and I pray that is so as we turn into 2013.*

That night, he finally slept. And in the morning he was brighter and lighter than he had been for weeks. He was able to meditate for the first time in a long while without being overcome by the screeching of his tinnitus. When he came down at breakfast he said, "That was the darkest night of my life and you pulled me through it. And this morning I was able to get beyond the ringing. I touched into the great wide peace that I have been missing in my meditation."

I asked him if I could record him on my iPhone. "This tinnitus will come and go," I said, "and I want you to say to yourself what you will need to hear when you are in a darker place."

He said into the iPhone, with his voice cracking, "Don't give up. Don't give up. Keep on breaking through . . . keep breaking open . . . keep giving it all up . . . surrender it all . . . to love . . . to love . . . love is all there is. Just keep on loving. Keep on loving. I don't know if I can do it . . . if I can keep going . . . but I know that love is everything . . ."

I have wondered since whether he was speaking these words to me and not really to himself. In any case, David never got to hear his words again. But I did. After he died I listened to this recorded message every day—many times a day. I played it for his sister, Pam, and to a few other friends. And strangely, at some point the recording simply disappeared from my phone. But the words were already in my heart, the path already laid out ahead of me.

I don't know if I can do it . . . if I can keep going . . . but I know that love is everything.

Chapter 3:

The Earthquake Hits

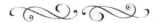

"To go in the dark with a light is to know the light.
To know the dark, go dark. Go without sight,
and find that the dark, too, blooms and sings,
and is traveled by dark feet and dark wings."

—WENDELL BERRY

It was now January 2, 2013, and all the family members and wedding guests were gathering from around the world for Claire and
Chris's wedding. That Wednesday evening, David and I drove into
Seattle for a celebratory dinner party with the clan at his sister's
home. It was the first of numerous planned events leading up to the
wedding day on Saturday.

In many ways, David was the life of the party. He was the one,
after all, who had brought these two young people together. The
oldest child of his dear sister, Pam, Claire was now a young woman
whom he had seen grow through the years. She had met Chris
through David Smith & Co, where they both worked.

After David had found his way to Indonesia and started to build
his teak business, Chris's father, James, had been instrumental in

helping him set things up. He'd guided David to grow his early passion with Indonesian antique folk art into a thriving business with a workshop in Java and a successful store in Seattle. James and David were loyal friends, and when James's son, Chris, was ready for a summer job, David hired him to work in his company and eventually he became his trusted store manager. Now, a few years later, we were about to celebrate the wedding of this young couple.

Claire and I had a special bond, and I was so thrilled to be a central part of this happy occasion with the family. Claire used to joke that they could never imagine David getting married until he met me. She used to be so mortified when she would go to a restaurant with him and he would ask for water with no ice, room temperature, with a slice of lemon. But when I did the same thing on a night out with her, she knew he had met his match. From early in our relationship, Pam's family had welcomed me into their tribe with open arms.

As we sat around the big oval table, faces all in pre-wedding glow, David stood up and made a touching toast with his signature blend of humor and meaning woven together spoken in his deep, resonant voice. He was strikingly handsome in his Indonesian handmade raw silk shirt, and for the first time in a while I saw the glimmer of life in his eyes that had gone out in the last few months. He spoke to the wonder of the mystery of life—first bringing him and James together years earlier, and now leading these young people to commit their lives to one another. Ultimately, it was a toast to the power of love. He was visibly moved, as were we all, and when he was done we clinked our glasses together with a cheer.

Only in hindsight could I see that this was David preparing us for his departure. His toast was a kind of goodbye in its acknowledgment of the love we all shared—a love we would need to call on in the hard days ahead after he was gone.

In the car on the way home that night, David said, "I had an amazing evening. This is the first time in months I haven't noticed my tinnitus, that it wasn't consuming all my attention."

We spoke about how this was the key to managing the situation—to not let his attention focus on the ringing but instead to orient toward others and the world. He seemed hopeful that he might be able to tame this crazy cacophony in his head, and I felt a sense of relief.

But that night he had a troubled sleep. He took Ambien before he went to bed, but it didn't seem to help; he tossed and turned for hours. Finally, he gave up trying to sleep and set off for a walk in the early-morning dark.

When I woke up and came down to the kitchen, he was a different man from the one I had cuddled up to when we went to sleep. It seemed to be a morning like many others, however, and I was busy with my preparations for leaving on the 8:15 a.m. foot passenger boat for Seattle. I will always regret that I did not take more time that morning to be present with him.

My last image of David alive is of him sitting stooped over the corner table of our kitchen in the darkness. He looked defeated. I asked him what he would do that day, and he did his best to perk up as he described a few things he had planned.

"Remember that there are bad days and good days," I said before leaving. "You told yourself that in the recording I made. You had a great time at the party last night. Why don't you make appetizers for when I get home tonight? We can sit in front of the fire and I will play you what I recorded you saying to yourself two days ago. Then we will cuddle up and watch *Downton Abbey*. We are going to get through this, honeybun."

He nodded his head slowly, agreeing with my plan—or so I thought.

I crossed over to where he was sitting and cuddled up next to him, and we kissed—not a sexual kiss but a slow, tender, and intimate sharing of love. I realized much later that it was his goodbye kiss.

I was uncomfortable with leaving David in this state of despair, but I had a ferry to catch. When I was almost out of the kitchen

I turned and said from across the room, "You aren't going to do anything stupid, are you? If you do I will never forgive you and I will find you in the afterworld and you will be so, so sorry." I was laughing while I said this, my conscious mind not believing he would ever take his life. And certainly not right before the big wedding.

But why did I even say that? What part of me did know that he could do that?

"Promise me?"

I stood glaring at him until he finally said, "Yes, I promise you." This was already a lie. He knew he was going.

———

On the ferry crossing over to Seattle, the sun was rising and it was turning into a gorgeous day. I texted David a photo of the beauty, along with my love.

He texted me back, *Beautiful day on island. Thinking of you with love.*

It was the last direct communication I would have from him. Later, it would occur to me that a text just two days earlier had said, *i love u deeply. me.* His last message was already distant; he had moved up into his head, distancing himself. He was now *thinking* of me.

———

The day was a whirl and swirl of activities with my two business partners. We were deep into preparations for the opening retreat of our first program in two years. Still, David was on my mind all day, and I texted him a couple of times—but never heard back.

This was unusual. Although he wasn't on his phone much, he was usually pretty good at responding to my texts. I could feel a little anxiety starting to brew in my belly.

On my way home, I called him on the home landline and on his cell—no answer. I was trying to hold it all lightly and stay calm, coming up with rational reasons he might not have answered—but by the time I drove down our driveway, my anxiety was gathering momentum. When I saw his car in the driveway, instead of being relieved I wondered why, if he was home, he hadn't answered my calls.

I literally ran down the path to the house and was met on the stone bridge crossing the water feature by my beloved cat, Emma. She was meowing, clearly wanting to get into the house. I wondered how she had gotten out, as I had locked the cat door—and why wasn't David letting her back in? This was definitely not good.

I called out David's name. No answer. I was starting to leave my body. My heart raced and my throat was dry as I charged from room to room—hoping to find him, afraid to find him dead. I was thinking a stroke or a heart attack, but also nagging in the background was the idea of suicide. But he was nowhere.

Dusk was turning into night as I went out to look farther around the property. Maybe he was in one of the many buildings on our land that he'd brought back from Indonesia, meditating. Maybe his phone was dead.

The part of me that had made him promise not to do anything stupid wondered if he might be in the building that had first brought him to this land. I held my breath as I entered the Kudus House— his sacred temple with elaborately carved teak walls and doors. But he wasn't there either.

By now I was starting to panic. I ran across the property and into what we called the Chinese House, another antique building from Java, this one with high ceilings and a spacious interior. As I called David's name, all I could hear was my voice echoing around the empty rooms. He was not there either.

Then I remembered that he had said he might visit with Antonia and Rob, our neighbors down the road. They weren't answering their phones, so I ran over to their house. They were hosting a friend for dinner and said that they had not heard from him. I told them how odd it was that he was not responding and that I was worried. It was very unlike him not to be home, especially since we had made a plan for the evening. He had learned over the years that this was what made me happy . . . to have wine and appetizers with him and connect after our day. This was not his language of love, it was mine. But he had learned it well. So this was definitely out of character.

Rob and Antonia, sensing my distress, came over to my house with me and we began to search together. I called my business partner and dear friend Deborah—one of the women I had just been working with all day—to tell her I was worried and she said, "I'm coming over." It didn't seem necessary for her to come, because I was still sure there was some reasonable explanation for his absence, but I didn't fight it.

Later she would tell me that she had an intuition when I told her that day that David was not responding to my texts that something was not right. On the way over she called my dear friend Sharleen, who had just flown from Seattle to Hawaii, to say she had a bad feeling about this. She called another friend, Sarah, who immediately got into her car to head to Vashon. Then she called Susan, my friend and business partner, who jumped in a car with her husband, David, and rushed to the ferry. They were the last people on the boat as it pulled away from the dock.

I called David's sister, Pam, to see if she had heard from him. Nothing.

I called Kevin, another friend he had been with recently, to see if he knew where he might be. I got his voice mail and left a message. An hour later, he called me back and said that he had not heard from David since the day before and that he and his wife were on a retreat at Mt. Rainier. He said they would come back to Seattle right away. I remember thinking that was odd, since I still felt David would appear any minute and his friends needn't worry so much.

Much later, I would learn from Kevin that during the last sauna they had taken together on January 1, David had talked with him about the different ways he had been considering taking his life. He'd spoken about it like it was something he had thought about in the past, however, and when Kevin had asked him if he was thinking of doing that now, he'd said he wasn't. But he had asked him to keep their conversation in absolute confidence—to not share anything with his wife or with me. When I reached him that night, the news resonated with a growing anxiety he already had about David taking his life.

I called David's best friend, Phil—the friend who had come with David to tour my house those many years earlier—to see if he had heard from him. He told me that they had spoken in the morning and David had been depressed. What he did not tell me then but told me later was that David had just received a letter from the Bank of America calling in a large business loan. He had called Phil in despair and said that he did not think he had the strength to carry on anymore . . . to keep his financial house of cards from falling down.

David had been juggling his financial overreaching for many decades, I would come to discover very soon—borrowing from one person to pay another. His obsession with creating his Vashon Island sanctuary had lured him far over the financial precipice time and time again. When the Bank of America loan was called in, he felt he had tipped over the edge of no return.

Later, Phil would also tell me he wished he had broken their confidentiality agreement and called me to say he was worried about David. Another of my dear friends would also later confess that David had spoken with him about researching hemlock as an agent for suicide. Again, he'd talked about it as a thing of the past and sworn him to silence. David had woven his web of secrecy well with his men friends, allowing him to do what he wanted while leaving them with an egregious legacy of guilt and shame.

I called another neighbor—Marcus, a longtime friend of David's—and he came over to help with the search. I also called David's brother, Greg, who lived near the ferry terminal in Seattle. I let him know that I was worried and that we were doing a search, and asked him to come and help.

By now it was 9:00 p.m. and something was definitely not right. But suicide was still not an option my mind would offer me. I wondered if he had a brain tumor that was causing the tinnitus. Was it possible that he had wandered off and was in trouble somewhere in the woods?

It was dark and I knew I would need help to do a larger search.

I made the decision to call the police.

It was a huge relief when Deborah, Susan, and her husband David showed up as reinforcements. It was all going to be alright. By now it had started to pour rain and everyone was out with flashlights in different corners of our large property.

I asked the two policemen who arrived if they could get more people to help with the search and they asked me an awkward question: "Did David have suicidal tendencies?"

The inquiry jolted me awake to the possibility of suicide—the thought that I had been suppressing until that moment. I told them what I believed was the truth: "He had suicidal thoughts in his younger years, but not since I have known him the past ten years."

That ended the option to add others to the search, as there was a policy against organizing a volunteer search party if the lost person had suicidal tendencies in order to protect young people in the group from the trauma of finding the body.

My friends asked me if I knew any psychics I could call who might be able to help with identifying David's location. I thought of Maleah, whom I had worked with before, and called her. Strangely, given how late it was, she answered the phone. I put her on speaker phone and, standing in my office with Deborah, Antonia, and Susan, I explained the situation.

She dropped into a meditation and then began to speak. "He is with an older woman," she said. "Everything is okay. He is a bit disoriented, but this woman is taking care of him. Do you know who this woman could be?"

Still holding the idea that he'd had had a stroke or something like that, I started to think of women in the neighborhood who could be looking after him.

"The woman is older and has a kind of pageboy haircut," Maleah said. "She is very kind and sweet."

I immediately thought of David's mother. But she was dead. Something clunked deep down in my belly as this thought passed through my mind.

"He is in a kind of place that looks like a town square," Maleah continued. "There are lots of large flagstones on the ground."

I could not think of where this might be. Later it would become clear that this was the stone platform David had built for a neighbor right beside where he died. He had shipped the beautiful big stones from Java for an outdoor Qigong space.

"I think the woman's name who is looking after him is Mary," Maleah said. "Do you know any Marys?"

I did not know any local Marys he could have walked to, but I again thought of his mother, whose name was Mary Ellen. But she had died almost exactly one year earlier. Unless . . .

Unless David is already dead and with her on the other side.

Just as this thought arose, Antonia got a call from her partner, Rob.

The color drained from her face.

"What is it?" I blurted out.

She stood frozen in place, momentarily unable to speak. And then—"Rob found David. He's at the neighbors'. He's dead."

With those final two words my life was shattered and I found myself standing in another world. I dropped my phone, Maleah still on the other end, and ran down our hallway screaming, my body impulse moving me somewhere—anywhere—away from those words.

"I have to go to him," I cried. "Let's go . . . now!"

Deborah grabbed her keys and we ran to the car. The police had heard me scream and came toward us as we climbed into the car. As we tried to pull out of the drive, they walked ahead of us so that we couldn't pass them.

I was a wild woman by now; my only goal was to get to my beloved first. I leapt from the car and started running through the pelting rain down the driveway. The police tried to stop me, saying it was a crime scene, but I was unstoppable and pushed past them.

Susan's husband David, a masters class long-distance runner and medalist in the USA, was walking with the police. I grabbed a hold of his arm and told him to run with me to the neighbors. He was Hermes the messenger God with wings on his heels. The two of us flew down our gravel driveway, over a bumpy field to the house next door. I do not know how we did it without breaking our ankles. I am not even sure our feet touched the ground.

It was pitch black and pouring rain.

Rob was standing beside the hot tub with a single flashlight. I could just make out his anguished face. He had covered the tub with some kind of tarp, not wanting me to see what was inside.

I threw it off.

In the dim light of Rob's flashlight, I could see David. He was half submerged, floating on his side quite peacefully, with his knees up by his chest like one might do floating in the ocean.

"We have to get him out of here," I shouted

Some wilderness rescuer part of me felt that I could still save him—or that I at least had to try. Like maybe if we got him out of the tub he would not be dead. Like maybe it was not too late.

Rob helped me to pull him from the tub and lay his body, frozen in a kind of fetal position, on its side. I would hear from my friends later that I howled an awful raw animal sound and called his name as I leaned over his body. I do not remember doing either of those things.

I do remember holding him . . . holding his hand . . . lying on my side next to him . . . telling him I loved him. I remember the rain, I remember the dark . . . I remember there was only the two of us.

And I remember knowing for sure that he . . . his spirit . . . my beloved soul partner . . . was not there.

I had never seen a dead body before; I had never felt this emptiness. I'd never understood before the way that a soul fills out the physical body with life force. I knew for sure that the one I loved was no longer there.

Later people would ask me if it was hard to see him dead. Yes, and there are some difficult flashback moments. But I needed to know that he was gone and that he wasn't coming back into the form I knew. I needed to see and touch that lifeless body to know his beautiful essence was somewhere else now.

Later my therapist would say to me that my running to try to save him was part of what allowed the trauma of the whole situation to move through my body more easily. Those who are not able to physically move through the energy of trauma have a much more difficult time releasing it from the body.

⸻

When the police finally arrived after finding their way through the woods to where we were, they took over the scene and called for reinforcements.

My attention shifted now from trying to save David to wanting to help him cross over to the other side. Now that this was a crime scene, the only thing I could do would be help him with the transition. Doing something was the main impulse. I had to do something, *anything*. I had to help my beloved somehow.

I was still convinced at this point that he'd had a stroke from the brain tumor that was causing his tinnitus. I would learn later that Deborah had seen the slits in his wrists and the ochre color of the water in the hot tub. My friends knew he had taken his life by this point but did not tell me. I am grateful for their sense of timing, as it allowed me to be in ritual space with David without the confusion the fact of his suicide would have caused me.

For the past two months before his death I had been putting myself through a kind of afterlife graduate school, seemingly preparing for just this moment. I had become obsessed with reading books about what happened when we died and crossed over to the other side. At night I would sit in bed reading *The Tibetan Book of Living and Dying*, *Journey of Souls*, and *Destiny of Souls*, comparing and contrasting perspectives. I would discuss these with David at night and he would always say, "Honeybun, you need to get some lighter reading material. How about some fiction?"

But I was obsessed and would finish one book and order another. Now I believe that some part of me was preparing for his death. Were there beings at other levels helping me, guiding me to do this? Did I know intuitively, unconsciously, that David was considering suicide?

Whatever the incentive, I was grateful for this understanding when the time came. I felt I knew where he'd gone and where I could not go just yet.

What I believed from my research was that the first few hours and days were critical for the soul as it transitioned out of the body, so I asked my friends to come back with me to the house and called my dear friend Sharleen, who had recently helped her mother transition through death. She had just arrived in Maui that day from Seattle, but upon hearing from me she said she would jump back on a plane the next day to return.

Sharleen and I had met right around the same time I met David, and we had been fast friends ever since. In a synchronous way, it turned out that the boathouse David had transformed into a teahouse on the water's edge, just a few doors away from my house, was owned by her sister Leone. Only a few years earlier, she had been present at her sister's death as well.

Over the phone, she patiently walked me through what to do with oil and how to care for the body after death. It never occurred to me then that I would not get David's body, since it was now part of a crime scene. It also never occurred to me that rigor mortis had already set in and that I wasn't going to be rubbing oil ritually on a body in a crouch position.

When I did finally discover that I would not be able to have the body, I asked my friends to come with me into David's office and do a ritual for his crossing-over.

It turned out that the friend that had been having dinner with Antonia and Rob earlier in the evening, Kim, was trained in a shamanic tradition specifically oriented to helping souls cross over after death, and she just happened to have her "mesa" with the sacred objects used in these rituals with her in her car—another synchronous event. I had never met her before but she generously agreed to facilitate the ritual.

David's small office on the second floor was his private temple, with a high, peaked ceiling and a rough-hewn stone fireplace. It was all windows, and he would sit in meditation or write for hours up there, looking out over the stunning view of the Puget Sound and the Olympic Mountains.

We lit candles, burned sage, and settled into the ceremony. Using her shamanic rattle, Kim set the circle for us, calling in the directions and the guiding spirits. And then, rattling in a counter-clockwise direction, she began to unwind all the chakras in David's body so that no part of his energy would be left behind as he traveled to the other side.

The scent of sage, the safety of being with my girlfriends, and the vibration of the rattling all lifted me out of my own body and into a place between the worlds. I was invited by Kim to speak to David.

"David my darling," I began, "my beloved . . . I release you to the light. I love you with all my heart. I have loved you through many lifetimes and I will always love you. You may go now from this earth, from this body. Go swiftly and with ease. You have lived a good life here. It is your time to go now. So be it."

Even as I said these things I had an image of him far away already, walking confidently toward the light. As though he knew what he was doing and where he was going. I saw him turn his head to look at me and smile, and then he kept on walking. Later, Kim would tell me that in all the rituals she had done over the years to help people cross over, this was the first time she had experienced a soul moving on so swiftly. Often they hung around earth confused, she told me.

David was not like that. He wasn't confused about leaving. He seemed to know how to make the transition and was on his way home.

When a psychic that I worked with years later channeled David, she told me that he had stayed longer than he had planned to, or that his soul had contracted for. He'd stayed because of his love for me. And then he'd simply been done. He had to go. The energetic gate had opened, and he'd taken it.

When we had completed the ritual, I felt relieved. At least I had done something. We returned downstairs, where the police were organizing the collection of the body and all of the other things that needed to be set in motion. In the kitchen, I noticed a few of my friends huddling with the police in some kind of intense conversation.

Once they had finished, my women friends came around me as I stood by the fire and Susan's husband, David, who had carried me on his arm to the hot tub earlier, was clearly the one chosen to speak. He had obviously gotten the short end of the straw. He asked me to sit down. I said no—I would stand.

"There is one more thing you need to know about David's death," he said, his eyes flicking from side to side like he didn't want to meet my gaze. "David . . . committed suicide." He looked down at the floor. "He slit his wrists."

In fact, as I would find out later, he did more than that. He had taken no chances that he would return from this suicide. This was not a "call for help" attempt. He had taken a full bottle of Ambien, gotten in the hot tub, and slit his wrists—a three-tiered approach to guarantee his exit. Ultimately, the death certificate reported that he had died from drowning.

His words could find no purchase in my mind. It was unbelievable. Unimaginable. Unacceptable.

When they did finally land, a fire rose up in me—I know not from where—and I spoke words that would set out the path I would travel for many years to come and am still traveling today: "I will not let this take me down. I will not let this destroy my life, my work. I will bring the Divine Feminine to the world. He will not take this with him. So be it!"

I next learned that David had written letters; his brother had found them in his car, in a brown paper Thriftway bag. It was so un-David-like to use a random paper bag. Perhaps he did not want me to find them when I first arrived home, to find the letters before I found his body. If that was his thought, I appreciate it. It was terrifying enough to be looking for him in the dark of the night—but at least then I was still holding out hope that he was out with a friend or, in the worst-case scenario, had experienced a stroke and was lying in the woods somewhere. The horror of looking for him knowing he was dead would have been too much.

Without telling me, his brother had given the letters to the police and they had taken them into custody as evidence. It was *letters*, plural—so who had he written them to and what had he said?

I was outraged that I could not have them! How did the police have the right to take the last intimate words of my beloved, someone they did not know at all, to some sterile office and read them first? I was horrified that some random policeman was reading his tender words to me before I could take them into my own heart.

It would not be until later the following day that the letters would finally be returned to me.

That night as I lay in my bed with Deborah and Sarah on either side of me and Emma at my head, I felt myself beginning to tip into another life. I knew that I had crossed over a threshold. There would be before and after this moment. I did not know how I would live through the after, but I knew in the depths of my being that I would find my way. When I awoke, what would become my new life would begin from this brutal, hallowed ground.

Chapter 4:

Descent into the Underworld

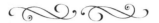

*"If a person wishes to be sure of the road they tread,
they must close their eyes and walk in the dark."*

—St. John of the Cross

I do not know if I slept at all that first night. I went in and out of
consciousness, and each time I awakened I had to push through
a fog of confusion about where I was and who I was with before
remembering—and then I was back in the horror of my own life and
the heavy blanket of grief dropped over me again. It was as though
the grief gestapo would back off when I was in the sleep state, but
once I was awake again they would grab me by the throat and slam
me up against the wall of reality, forcing me to face the devastation
of my life. This would be the case for many, many mornings to come.

Some kind of community mechanism that I will never truly
understand but always deeply appreciate went into full gear that first
night. People were called, and they jumped into their cars and set
off for Vashon or turned cars around and headed home from trips
away. Flights out of Seattle were canceled; flights into Seattle were
booked. People arrived with various food offerings, dropping them

with cooking instructions on the front step. Friends crept quietly down the long front path toward the house—wanting to be there but wondering if they should be, not knowing how to show up for me in the midst of this impossible reality.

And while all this was going on, I was transported into some alternate bardo—a kind of in-between place that trauma escorts you to. The gap between my life the day before—the me who was living her dream life, preparing to launch her first book and new program into the world—and the me now, whose beloved husband had just committed suicide, was just too wide to comprehend.

At first I tried to find my way back into my old reality. Like there must be a way out of this nightmare—if I could just figure out the path. Denial is the brake that our nervous system engages during trauma to avoid blowing out all our circuits when the situation is too overwhelming. Acceptance comes bit by bit as we are able to bear the truth of the devastation.

My dear circle of women friends quickly took up residence at my house. Plans were being made, food was being cooked, systems were being set in motion. I remember walking downstairs the morning after David's death and seeing everyone busy—answering doors and phones, directing people here and there—like bees in a hive protecting the queen. And I thought, *How odd that this drama is happening to me.* It was like I was outside of myself, looking at the scene with the sense that the wrong character was playing the leading role. I was the one with the perfect life—living with my beloved husband on our beautiful sanctuary estate on a tranquil island, doing the work I loved to do, about to launch myself back into the world after years of writing.

I was not the heroine of a tragedy. This was a total miscasting.

I drifted into the kitchen where my friends were gathered, and everyone stopped talking as all eyes turned toward me. I could not shake off this sense that I was not meant to be the leading lady, and some part of my mind kept scrambling to reject this role. As though if I didn't accept it, the drama could not continue. There was a part of me watching myself do this—not settling into the reality of what had happened—and recognizing that this was a healthy trauma response. And I also knew that acceptance of "what is" was going to be very important for me.

For many years I had coached women through deep change processes, and the first step was always to anchor the capacity *to be with what is*—to be fierce with reality and be able to accept the situations we find ourselves in. So much unnecessary suffering comes from resisting the change that is trying to work its way through us. I knew there was enough suffering in this situation on its own without adding my resistance to it.

My first test came when I finally received the letters David had written. There was one for me; one for his sister, Pam; one for the bride-to-be, Claire; and one for his longtime assistant and dear friend Carol.

I sat for a long time on the end of our bed with the envelope in my hand. I knew that suicide letters could be hard for those left behind. I hoped that he would explain everything in a way that would help me make sense of this insane nightmare, or at least maybe give me a thread of connection that I could follow through the darkness I knew lay ahead.

My friend Sarah sat quietly next to me with her hand on my back. My heart was pounding, and I was barely able to breathe. David had chosen a big square card for me with the head of a reclining Buddha propped up on one arm looking out serenely at white clouds floating across a blue sky beyond. An image of such peace and letting go. In a strange coincidence (or not), the card was from a company called Mr. Smith.

I read each word slowly—out loud, so that I could hear them reverberating. My body shaking, tears streaming down my face. I lost myself for a while inside these words . . . reading them over and over again. I wanted to hear the gentle rumble of his voice carrying all the love and despair contained in the words . . . I wanted not to be *reading* them.

Most of the people who had come to the house so far were my friends, not David's close connections, but shortly after I had read the letter I looked out the window and saw Stephen, an old and very dear friend of David's, coming down the pathway to the house. I dropped what I was doing, bolted out of the room, and ran down the path to grab him. He was the closest thing I had to David right now, and I needed him.

"What happened?" I asked him. "How could David do this? Please help me understand this nightmare." I wanted Stephen to make sense of the horror.

"I am so, so sorry," he said in barely a whisper. "I know David has had difficult moments in the past, but I can't understand this either. I don't know . . . I don't know . . ." His eyes brimmed over with tears.

We talked together for a while, close and quiet . . . like we were in church. Speaking to someone who had known David much longer than I had and who also loved him was comforting. I was starting to drop down into the burning coals of loss.

It was clear that this fire was hotter than anything I had ever experienced before in my life, and I would need help to step into it. I knew just who to call—my friend and ritual elder Michael Meade. I remembered how we had recently spoken about his working with local high school students after a suicide trauma. We had also spent the past year in conversations about creating a ritual theater performance of the Greek Persephone-Demeter myth, in which the God of the Underworld Hades grabs innocent Persephone and drags her into his realm, kicking and screaming, where she ultimately wakes up to her full embodied nature and becomes queen of both the Underworld and the Upper World. It was a guiding story in the transformational work I did with women, a story of loss, deep change, and rebirth.

I felt sure Michael would know something about how to go forward across the barren landscape of loss and help me to accept the tragic role I'd found myself in. I called him then, that first day after David's death, and he agreed to come right away.

When Michael arrived, I took him up to our bedroom—it was the only truly private space with a door in the house, and I wanted to speak to him frankly. There was nowhere to sit but the bed, and I realized as soon as I motioned for him to sit down that this was too intimate a space. But it was all that we had, so I just kept moving through the awkwardness.

I told him everything I knew so far—which was not very much. And I read him the letter David had written to me before he died. I think I hoped that he would make sense of it all—have something wise to say that would steady me and arrest my freefall.

Instead, his words encouraged me to let go.

"This is probably the biggest Hades grab you will ever experience," Michael said, speaking each word slowly and looking me straight in the eyes, "but remember that you are Queen Persephone and you know how to navigate in the dark. Surrender now and let the descent take you where it must. Others will hold space for you in the Upper World."

I remember those words—and the way in which they burned through the fog and confusion of all that was being swept away—like they were spoken yesterday. For a moment, the mist parted, and I could see the path heading down into the darker realms.

To embrace the dark and the light, to be with the mystery and step boldly into the unknown, was something I had been guiding women toward for decades. Now I would step forward myself to the edge of darkness. I bowed my head and said to myself, *YES, I will make my path by walking—I will not resist.* As those words found shape in my consciousness, I felt the slightest lifting of something in my heart—a hope that I would one day reemerge from the dark to which I was about to surrender. And then down I went.

From that moment onward I understood there was nowhere to go, nowhere to hide from the darkness that was calling for me. I knew not to resist this Hades grab. My identity and my future cleaved away in front of me like a giant iceberg breaking free. David's unexpected and chosen death brought me to my knees in a way that I cannot imagine any other act doing.

There are times in a life when the shattering is so complete that all one can do is bow down and honor the threshold. The past is gone, the future completely unknown, and the only step you can take is to acknowledge the groundless ground between these worlds that you now stand on.

Even now when I think back to that time, I cannot equate all that occurred to any kind of normal sense of hours and minutes. Trauma seems to knock out that linear organizing principle. I had only the present moment available. The past was way too triggering to recall—not only David's death but also any moments of closeness and love before that. And the future was obscured completely—a foggy sense of uncertainty and dread were all that I saw ahead.

At the end of the first day after David's suicide, January 4 , I wrote in my WeMoon journal: *I begin a new calendar with a new life. David is dead and I am in free fall . . . it is the hardest time of my life . . . I will make it through . . . day by day I guess . . .*

When I finished writing those words and fell into bed, I knew only this:

The positive reframe part of me had been annihilated—there was nothing good I could make of this situation.

The innocent part of me was brutally torn asunder—my fundamental belief that bad things don't happen to good people had been hung out to dry.

The spiritual bypass part of me was disabled—I knew I would have to go through this journey in my humanness. Ever since I'd knelt beside David's body and felt the certainty of his death, I'd known I would not leave my body or my feelings behind.

The heroic part of me was shattered—I could only do what I could do each day going forward, and whatever I did it would have to be authentic.

My confidence that I could handle anything life threw at me was gone. I did not know if I could get through this without going crazy or losing everything.

While I had no certainty that things would work out or that I would make it through the dark night I was entering, there was one more thing I knew with absolute certainty: I was being called to practice what I taught, to live into all that I had guided myself and so many women to become. I would walk through this in the Way of the Mysterial Woman. I would find out firsthand whether this updated inner operating system could hold up as one turned into the galeforce winds of their fate.

A Mythic Journey

Part III

And so one day, as the winter sun sank low on the horizon, the king left his beloved and his magical kingdom, quietly slipping out of this world and over into the next.

The sky wept at his death, and where there was once sun now there were only dark clouds and pelting rain. The queen and all her allies searched high and low for him and finally they found his lifeless form floating in the water. Using all her strength, she pulled him out and fell over his empty shell of a body, letting out a howl that was heard in all the realms. The grand order of the kingdom had been shattered.

When later she heard that it was by his own hand that he had died, leaving her alone with the collapsing kingdom, a goddess strength rose up in her. She stood tall in front of the fire and, with her friends bearing witness, she spoke her vows: "I will not be taken down by your brutal act. I will do what needs to be done to mend this tear in the fabric of life. And I will be the one who can walk through the fire of transformation. So be it!"

And with those words she turned into the winds of her fate, determined to live for both of them.

Her path was harsh, as the vultures came quickly to pick from the carcass of her dead husband's creation. She bravely fought them off one at a time until there was some order again in the realm. When that task was done, she knew that she would leave the kingdom and follow her own path into the world. Until then, she would make her path by walking.

Part Two:

Initiation

Introduction to the
Mysterial Meta-Capacities

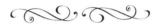

In the moment of my tumbling down into Hades, I knew that surrender was essential. I was not thinking about engaging all the archetypes of the powerful Mysterial work that I had done for decades with women. My prefrontal cortex, which primarily holds the executive function of orchestrating thoughts and actions, was mostly offline through the initial phase of the trauma, and I trusted that the capacities I would need were already embodied.

The challenge that lay ahead for me was to fully live into the Mysterial way—something that I had never test-driven in such extreme conditions. In the final chapters of *The Way of the Mysterial Woman*, we described the eight Mysterial Meta-Capacities that we were just starting to see arising in women who had done the transformational work of clearing the shadows and cultivating the strengths of the five primary Feminine and Masculine archetypes women embody in a sequence as they develop: Mother, Hero, Father, Maiden, and Crone.

I had seen the blueprint for a fundamentally new way of being in the world—but I did not know for sure if it could actually be fully lived out in the most challenging circumstances possible. I was the mapmaker who had charted a route to a possible new land, but had never explored further than the beachfront. I had an image of what this woman of the future, who was emerging now in the present and would lead us through these dark times, looked like. And that image, burned into my soul, became an important guiding light for me in my descent.

Through the next chapters, I will show you my initiation into the lived experience of each of the eight Meta-Capacities of a Mysterial Woman that I drew upon during my journey: Multi-Dimensional Knowing, Embracing Paradox, Authentic Presence, Energy Stewardship, Dynamic Mutuality, Tending the Field, Influencing System Resonance, and Unfolding the Emergent.

These capacities, newly arising from an expanded consciounsenss, are an evolutionary response to the complexity of the world today. I will explain each capacity in much greater depth as you walk with me into them one by one. At the beginning of each chapter, I will give you a brief definition of the Meta-Capacity I will be highlighting. Evolutionary invocations open each Meta-Capacity, and I invite you to use your imagination to conjure up an image of what it might be like if you fully embodied that capacity as a woman on the edge of evolution. In these invocations you may recognize word fragments from different poems I used during my journey; I am deeply grateful for the path poetry offered me through the darkness. (You will find more about the power of poetry as a healing vessel in the resources section at the end of this book.) Finally, I will dive into a story that will help you to see how the embodiment of each capacity expressed itself through me.

In reality, my experience of the eight Meta-Capacities was that they were all co-arising in the midst of each challenging circumstance, but I have tried to separate them out here so that you can get a sense for each of them individually. I believe it was my testing them and daily calling upon them that not only got me through the days and years following David's death, but also got me through in a way that left me profoundly changed and more authentically myself. I believe they are what we need now to walk through our personal and collective traumas. They are the capacities that are emerging in culture to help us heal our pasts and not only make it through the turbulent, shaky, changing times we are living in but ultimately actually enable us to give birth to the next level of our potential as a human species.

Nothing less than everything was at stake for me as I set out to make my path by walking.

Chapter 5:

Meta-Capacity —
Generative Mutuality

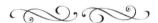

Generative Mutuality is an essential capacity to address the challenges we are all facing in a world of increasing complexity, disruption, and uncertainty. Breaking the words down, it means to be committed to being undefended, curious, and compassionate with oneself and others (Mutuality) so that collaborative and creative solutions to conflicts and very hard problems can be found (Generative). It is built on a foundation of integrity and self-awareness so that our relationships can withstand the inevitable storms of reactivity that naturally arise in difficult conversations. It means resisting old beliefs about being alone in a hostile world, and instead having the capacity to stay connected to what is true for you while being genuinely open to another person's perspective.

One thing that was crystal clear to me from the beginning of my journey was that I could not move through this trauma alone. I would need to bring as much of myself as possible into relationship with all of the others who were so devastated by David's suicide. In order to make my way through the chaos, I would need to be transparent, open, and deeply compassionate. I would need to find a new relationship with my fear of not belonging and keep remembering that I was not alone and that I was part of a "friendly universe."

An Evolutionary Invitation:
Generative Mutuality

Meditate on the words below and let them evoke your body, heart, mind, and soul. Imagine yourself as a woman on the edge of evolution expressing Generative Mutuality.

The illusion of separateness falls away
Control is relinquished for surrender into something larger
As you rest into the cosmic web of life
Feeling the thrum of interbeing

You are at home in your adult aloneness
And naturally belong
Opening into the intimacy of communion from this fullness
Setting the other free to be themselves
Not reducing the poetry of their being to your stale prose

You dowse for the water of truth in the wespace between
And when you find it you bravely drink from this aquifer
Trusting that what is so now is the ground for what will come later

Undefended and curious, you lean neither
Toward nor away from the other
Choosing to stand in the spacious place of presence
As you allow the mystery of mutuality to unfold naturally

Sacred Wedding in Darkness

In the early days and hours following David's death, my capacity for Generative Mutuality was gratefully onboard and I kept inviting those who were called to help to come in close. My home became a beehive of activity as friends and family cooked meals, cleaned, sorted through finances, held me, fed me, and surrounded me in love. Something greater than me was forming in the collective field of this trauma, and I could feel it.

I was also aware of David's family across the water in Seattle and I knew they must also be in enormous grief and chaos. Could Claire and Chris's wedding go forward in the midst of this horrific tragedy? David was the one who had brought them together—it was only the night before that he had toasted both of them and their two families with such gusto. He was the one who had spoken about the amazing mystery of life bringing people together, and about how love is all there is.

Ultimately, the two families made the difficult decision that they would go forward with the wedding. Chris's family had come from Indonesia and Australia and all the plans had been made, the event spaces paid for, the bride and groom ready for marriage. There was too much to lose at every level to cancel—and yet how would everyone hold this sacred union alongside such death and despair? Each of us would need to answer that question for ourselves.

The strength and resilience of this young couple was remarkable. They chose to walk through their broken-open hearts toward one another. (Even more remarkably, when they had their first child two years later, they named him Alex David.)

For me it was one event at a time, and I had to decide what I could actually manage. The fearless part of my nature that got me through many difficult situations and losses in the past was shattered. This hypermasculine, heroic, "push through anything" force I had inherited from my father was simply gone. Every important step forward I would do only if I authentically could. Moment by moment, I asked myself if the action being called for was mine to do. Generative Mutuality is not about saying *yes* to everything—it is about knowing what the correct action for you is, and trusting that others know the same for themselves.

One of the first challenges would come as I faced toward the wedding and the impossible task of being present while the specter of David's death was still all around me.

The rehearsal dinner was scheduled for Friday evening in Seattle, and after speaking with David's sister, Pam, I decided I would at least come into the city for a meeting at her house with the two families and the ministers—a couple who would perform the wedding. They had offered to hold a gathering with Claire and Chris's immediate family before the dinner, and I knew this would be essential for Generative Mutuality. It would be good for me to be there with everyone, even though it would be hard. My friend Sarah, who was staying with me on Vashon, drove me in and was by my side for the rest of the night.

There were many tears as we greeted each other for the first time since the celebratory dinner—all of us in a state of absolute shock. Words were not yet possible for the horror that had occurred, and so we just sat close to one another in a throbbing silence.

The ministers did a beautiful job of holding a sacred space for extending prayers to David for his journey onward and offering blessings to the bride and groom. They spoke of how we might be with all of this in the ceremony the next day—how they would include something about his death while still orienting the service toward love and the beginning of new life. It felt good to be in a quiet ritual space with everyone.

I let go a bit more into the steadying hands of the ministers. If they could hold all this, then maybe I could too. This was a beautiful example of Generative Mutuality in action. They brought us into a field of love, reminding us that we could get through this together.

When we were done, everyone began to head out to the rehearsal dinner. I hadn't planned on attending, but I could feel that after our little service I had the energy to go if it would be appropriate for Claire and Chris. I was in the awkward position of wondering if I was a liability or an asset now. Would I remind everyone of what had happened and make it worse, or would my presence be a gift that sent the message that love prevails?

Ultimately, I decided that it would be easier for all the friends and family close to Claire and Chris who would be at the rehearsal dinner if they saw me before the wedding—that it might convey a message that I was okay, that we were all going to get through this, and that I was supporting their choice to go ahead with the wedding amidst such unbearable loss.

⁓

I entered the rehearsal dinner space with Sarah close at my side. I felt as though I was walking though a fog. . . like there simply was no ground under my feet. It was all surreal. Everyone was dressed beautifully, music was playing softly, and there was the clink of glasses and hum of chatting as people milled about.

In trauma, the sensory system is the dominant way of reading the world, as the prefrontal cortex is mostly offline. In the days after David's death, I was super sensitive to every sound and movement; it was as though my skin had been peeled back and I'd been left to engage with the world completely raw.

I could see that everyone was simultaneously trying to find a way to be in the joy of the upcoming wedding *and* integrate the brutality of what had happened. These two energies were moving in the space together, and they created an uncomfortable tension.

I made my way through the room, meeting everyone as if in slow motion. My tongue was heavy in my mouth and words were few. Mostly I just held people's hands and said something about Claire and Chris and their love for one another. And their courage.

I stayed long enough for the toasts and imagined what I might have said if I could have stood up in the midst of my trauma: "I am so grateful that I am able to stand here tonight to acknowledge Claire and Chris and their love for one another. I stand here for

David and for myself . . . and I honor the love that is here in this room tonight. Love is all there is. And it will get us all through these most difficult days. To Love."

———

Sarah and I sat in silence on the way home in the car that night. She knew when to speak and when to just be present with me.

When I got back to the house, my nephew Justin was there. He was the first of my family to arrive after David's death—and of course he was. He was the heart whisperer of the family. The kind of kid who would actually ask his aunt how she was and then listen to her answer—and then ask a relevant follow-up question to go deeper.

Since he was a little boy, when the adults would kick back from the table after an extended family dinner and start to tell stories, Justin would go quiet. You could almost see his little ears silently rotating toward whomever was speaking to make sure he didn't miss anything. He was the young man who risked his life and hiked for miles across difficult terrain to save the life of someone who had fallen off a cliff while hiking along the Great Wall of China. He was both a guy's guy and a girl's guy. As an outdoor adventure teacher, he was a strapping six feet, with strong arms, blond hair, and piercing blue eyes. He could climb, hike, bike, and ride wild horses over any terrain. But he was also the kind of guy that girls wanted for a best friend, because he was so damn understanding and he knew how to give those real hugs that convey, "I am glad to see you and you matter to me."

He'd been en route from Toronto back to Thailand, where he lived, when he'd heard the news about David's suicide. I could almost picture him breaking into the cabin of his Air Canada plane and saying, "My totally cool uncle David—the one I once told I wanted to model my life after—has just killed himself, and I need you to turn this plane around right now and head to Seattle so that I can be with my aunt Suzanne." All I knew was that he'd somehow arrived at my house less than twenty-four hours after this nightmare began, and was now wrapping me in his bear hug. Justin to the rescue. I remember feeling for just a moment that perhaps I was going to be okay. Justin would fix this unimaginable thing. Put the genie back in the bottle. Make it all go away. Justin had that effect on people.

Then the next wave of panic came rolling in.

But Justin stayed by my side, and for the first few days he was my unwavering rock.

I heard later that when he did the first family Skype session with my siblings who lived all around the globe he said, "Okay, family, this is a true shit show! We are all going to be needed. David's suicide has set off a financial tsunami and we haven't even begun to see the first big wave come in yet."

Truer words have never been spoken.

⎯⎯⎯⎯⎯⎯

The next day was the wedding, and like everything else I could not see very far into the future or whether I would have the strength to attend. With Justin, Sharleen, and Sarah present now, I felt able to go. But no one had fancy clothes with them, and I didn't know what I could possibly wear either. Everything nice that I had reminded me of David. I needed a dresser.

Lynda, a good friend of mine, had been in touch and offered to help in any way I needed. She immediately came to mind. She was an amazing artist, and her fabulous sense of style had always been very aligned with my own. We often laughed about how we could so easily swap closets and be happy in each other's clothes. So now, faced with the dilemma of what to wear to the wedding, I called her and asked if she could dress me, Sharleen, and Sarah. She didn't hesitate to say yes to my unusual request; in the spirit of Generative Mutuality, she jumped right in her car with a wide assortment of clothes.

Within three hours, she'd managed to get the ferry to the island, dress us all, and send us off to Seattle to the wedding.

I wore blood red, wide-legged silk pants from Thailand with an elegant wraparound blouse. Sharleen had on an embroidered coat from Cambodia with black pants. Sarah was elegant in a simple dress. Justin did his best with the clothes that he had with him.

Arriving at the event space early with the rest of David's family was so confusing for me. I had never been with them without him, and it just felt wrong. I was like an awkward schoolgirl on the first day of class, not knowing where to go or where I belonged now.

When the family had all arrived, the wedding photographer started gathering everyone for photos. They all followed him into a special room and a wave of terror gripped my heart. I grabbed my two girlfriends and ran to the bathroom, where I bent over in a mild panic attack. What was I doing here? Forty-eight hours earlier, my whole life had been different. If David was here, he and I would be right there in the midst of the family photos, no question. David would be laughing and joking with everyone and being his charming self. And I would be his beloved partner.

Now, however, I was the wife of the dead man who had just brutally killed himself mere days before his niece's wedding. I wasn't sure I could go back out there. The all-too-familiar, limiting belief of *"I do not belong"* had grabbed me by the throat and I was gasping for air.

This was a familiar feeling that had been activated in my early life by my challenging relationship with my father and would often kick in when I felt vulnerable in relationships.

I was a "father's daughter" if ever there was one. From as early as I can remember, I wanted to be seen, approved of, and loved by my father. He was a larger-than-life patriarch in our family—scientist, academic professor, leader, university president—with a ferocious sense of ambition and the accompanying drive and capacity to leave his mark on the world. And this he has done.

From my early years, I shaped myself around him. Eager for his acknowledgment, I became a great skier like he was, and tried my hand at every kind of accomplishment at school. I was curious about the world—and I wanted to make a difference. Just like my father, I was constantly in motion. And yet with all that achieving, it was rare that I ever felt the warm glow of his approval. His "no news is good news" approach to giving positive feedback left me hungry for some sign of his recognition and confirmation that I belonged. I understand today that he expressed his love for his family by working hard and achieving the success that allowed us to live comfortable lives of privilege. But at the time his absence from my life left me with a deep grief and growing anger at his inability to see me.

My old self-soothing strategy was to push down my need to belong and just go off on some independent adventure—basically, to run away as fast as I could. But I knew I could not do that here.

My friends rubbed my back and spoke kind words of support as they *gentled* me back into my body. In my programs, we connected this limiting belief with The Father archetype and I'd taught women who struggled with it how to start embracing the liberating belief, *"I am at home in myself and naturally belong."* I knew that I could call on this new possibility for myself, and after a few minutes I was able to breathe through the feelings, stand up, look at myself in the mirror, and affirm my version of these words out loud—"I am okay, I am loved, I do belong." I put on my lipstick, took a deep breath, and, with my girlfriends at my side, stepped out of the bathroom and back into the fray.

"Suzanne, where have you been?" David's nephew Peter said as soon as he saw me. "We are taking family photos. Come on."

"I wasn't sure you would want me in the photos," I said, my voice cracking. The truth was that I also wasn't sure I could endure standing up in the photos by myself.

"Of course we do, come on!" Peter said firmly.

I was numb inside but somehow managed to smile and be present for what seemed like an interminable period of time. I felt like a pariah—like I was a harbinger of death and destruction. My throat was swollen shut with the sobs that would not come until I headed home hours later.

The photographer was directing people into various configurations and at one point, so he could know what groups to put people into, he pointed at me and asked rather sharply of Claire, "Who is the woman beside you in red?"

I will never forget Claire's strong words: "She is my aunt."

In that moment, I felt her draw me into the family—even as the shame of what David had done and the pain he was causing hovered around me like a low-lying fog. She wanted me there. She was claiming me as family.

———

When the photos were complete, I got ready to go into the wedding hall with my nephew and friends. I was planning to sit at the very back with them and be invisible, if possible. Later, I realized how strange it was that I cast myself out of the family so quickly—like David's violent act had also sliced me from the family tree.

Pam approached me gently to ask if I would like to walk down the aisle with her and Peter. We were all making this up as we went along and figuring it out as it unfolded. I just wanted to be at the back of the room and somehow get through this without breaking down. But I could see the wisdom in what Pam was asking; my walking down the aisle with them was a way to let everyone there know that we were okay as a family and that I was very much blessing this union. It was also a way for Pam to bring me in close, and for Claire and Chris to feel me with them. This was another beautiful example of Generative Mutuality in action. I was present and available for connection, as was Pam. Looking back, I feel sure that our presence together was a healing force for others.

I do not know how we all managed that walk. How Peter, who adored his uncle, was able to hold up his devastated aunt, who had lost her beloved, on one arm and his mother, who had lost her oldest and dearest friend and brother, on the other.

And then we all sat in the front row together. David's death had blown open everything, and we were all the survivors trying to bless this union amidst all the other confusing emotions—grief, anger, fear, shame. Tears streamed down my cheeks, hot and unstoppable.

The archetypal moment of the bride's arrival shifted all of us as we turned our attention toward her. Claire appeared with her father at the end of the room, and we all rose up to our feet with our eyes and hearts locked onto the innocent bride in white, arriving to meet her beloved. But the innocence had been shattered—which made it all the more extraordinary that Claire could walk so steadily across the burnt ground of death, so fresh we could still all smell it, with hopes for a future with her beloved that would be more kind than the present.

Chapter 6:

Meta-Capacity—

Unfolding the Emergent

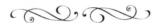

Unfolding the Emergent is the profoundly important capacity for listening to what is trying to emerge, even if it goes against the planned or expected outcomes. It means becoming comfortable with uncertainty and being willing to walk a path through the liminal spaces of not knowing, all the while paying attention to signals, synchronicities, and the sacredness of life. As a women's leadership facilitator, I had already started to see this Meta-Capacity in action, as my students began to allow themselves to let go of old, rigid structures, businesses, and relationships that no longer served them and step onto unknown paths that were inviting them forward.

A kind of dynamic steering is involved, where you are present in the moment while also tuning in to the next essential thing you must pay attention to. You focus on the most immediate tensions that need to be resolved, avoiding trying to make the *best* decision. When we are traumatized, we often think that we must immediately figure everything out with our minds to escape perceived danger. But with our nervous systems overwhelmed, the focus should not be on the grand plan but rather on the simple next step forward. Unfolding the Emergent allows us to meet a future that is not predicted along some linear path—it makes room for the mystery and the hidden wholeness to show itself.

I knew from day one of life without David that the only way through the devastation would be to dynamically steer in a very emergent way. I would have to be open to ambiguity and not knowing so that things could unfold along a path that I certainly couldn't see yet. I would need to be awake to the internal and external factors of the situation as they arose, paying close attention to subtle signs and coincidences, adjusting in the moment to take the next best step. To Unfold the Emergent I would need to honor rhythms and cycles, knowing that some things would require patient gestation and others would require quick and decisive action, even if it meant reassessing my original intention and changing course. I would need to be willing to let things dissolve and also discern the timing for when to bring things into a new synthesis.

An Evolutionary Invitation:
Unfolding the Emergent

Meditate on the words below and let them evoke your body, heart, mind, and soul. Imagine yourself as a woman on the edge of evolution Unfolding the Emergent.

Everything, every single thing unfolds in the grace of time

You remove what blocks the flow and gasp in
Delight at what is revealed
Before your innocent eyes

Visualizing your clear desire out ahead in the future
You surrender to how you journey there
Following the path seen and then not seen
You walk hand in hand with the mystery

Parts of you travel far ahead of your fears
Willing to not know, to pay attention to signs and signals, to let
Some things go and others emerge, to be surprised by life

What moves you comes from the heart of wonder
Not a stranger here on this good earth
You are a co-creator unfolding
A world of beauty and possibility

The Tsunami Hits

A high-magnitude earthquake near or under the water will typically trigger a tsunami that slams into and devastates the shoreline. And that is certainly how David's suicide played out for me. I clearly and consciously chose the Unfolding Emergent path as I stepped into the complete unknown. Losing my husband had already shaken me to the core. But it was the tsunami that swept in afterward that destroyed everything in my world. Even if I had wanted to cling to the familiar structures of my life, I couldn't—within days, it was clear I would lose everything.

The tsunami set off by David's suicide brought new flotsam and jetsam to my door on a daily basis, wave after wave. Just as I was getting my feet under me after one assault, the next would arrive.

After I made it through Claire and Chris's wedding, the next wave to hit was the unfathomable financial collapse that David's business was already well into.

The Bank of America calling in his large business loan was probably what tipped the scales for him, but the whole house of cards had already been coming down. Not that I knew the fullness of that until after he was gone. I was not privy to David's business operations, and although I'd known that he struggled with cash flow, as any retail business did, I had not been aware of the amount of debt he had generated over the years. I had my own business and was focused on relaunching a new women's leadership program and new book out into the world. I just didn't see this wave coming.

I knew that David's business went through stressful cycles, but he always seemed to handle them so well: he would disappear up to his study to meditate, and when he returned—aglow from the non-dual states he accessed—he had figured out a solution. We had agreed the year before to list our property and see what kind of response we could get. But our hearts weren't really in it. And David's certainly was not. There had been a few little nibbles, but no bites.

Two days after the wedding, while David's friend James and his family were still in town, we had a meeting at Pam's house. Along with all of them was my nephew Justin, so competent during crisis, and he facilitated the meeting, while his father, Brian, an accomplished executive, joined us by Skype. Carol, David's long-time business assistant and the person from whom he had borrowed the most money, and her partner, Claudia, were also at the table.

It was a grim gathering. As far as I could tell, the main objective was to stabilize as much as we could amid the tsunami set off by David's suicide. Justin and Brian were the ones in charge, and they conveyed exactly this message. They were strong and steady and basically letting everyone know that I would do my best to manage this situation. We would get through this if we did it together.

When a few days later Brian and my sister Hannah arrived from the East Coast, Brian put on his "let's get shit done hat" and started to pull the pieces of David's collapsing business into order. I began to see where I needed to start in order to unravel this mess.

By the time he left a week later, my brother-in-law had created a roadmap for me, making it clear what I had to attend to and by when. This was a necessary structure to help me Unfold the Emergent.

It took everything I had to think any rational thoughts. I did not have the luxury of lying in bed staring at the ceiling. I needed to assess things, make key decisions, and act on them swiftly. I was requiring my brain to operate in ways that it was not programmed to do during trauma. It was exhausting, and I was very grateful for those who stepped in to hold this function with me in the early days.

I knew that it was essential that I bring some order and structure to all the swirling chaos. At the same time, I wanted to run away and let someone else take care of everything. A voice inside tried to convince me that I was not equipped to sort out the financial world that my very business-oriented husband had not been able to figure out. I resisted this pull to numb out and wait to be rescued. Instead, I reached out for help so that I could stand in my own true authority and, step by step, make my way through the darkness.

The extraordinary thing was that a team of friends and family was naturally gathering around me and all I had to do was keep saying *yes* to the offers of help. This was in itself a new move for me, as my role in life had always been as the helper and healer—the one who gave, even overgave, to others. I knew that my real lesson and task was to open to the receptive Feminine and allow some coherence to form naturally out of the chaos. I also knew I could not do this on my own.

It was David's inability to face his crumbling world, ask for help, and turn toward the mess he had created that had brought me to this moment. I would do something different.

This opening to a force larger than oneself is a critical component of Unfolding the Emergent. Doing this is what allowed my center to hold—against the tempests of anger and betrayal, against the overwhelming weight of grief and despair, against the disorienting fogs of confusion, against the uncontrollable waves of fear that left me trembling and spent at the end of many days.

Like the statue of the Virgin Mary at Breezy Point in Queens, NY—left miraculously untouched after Hurricane Sandy when everything else around her was battered down by the force of the winter storm—my center held. There in the midst of the wreckage of my life was the vessel of my soul's presence, very much intact, and I stayed lashed to its mast through the tumultuous months that followed. There were times when the waves of the trauma were so large that I thought I would never reemerge from the valley of the swell. There were also times when everything was so still and breathless that I could not . . . did not want to . . . imagine a future without David.

All certainty was erased—even the certainty that my center would hold. I did not know. This is the ecology of trauma: it is a barren and unfamiliar world—unpredictable, raw, and dangerous. This is also why our capacity for Unfolding the Emergent is so crucial in navigating through the turmoil of trauma and loss. In my case, all I knew was that I had to keep opening the doors and allowing the path forward to reveal itself one step at a time.

And so when Rick, the husband of my dear friend and colleague Julia, offered to bring his expertise as a forensic accountant to the "Shit Show" team, as Justin had named it, I said *yes*—though I didn't even know what a forensic accountant did. It turned out they use their accounting skills to investigate fraud, embezzlement, and other irregularities hidden as financial transactions in businesses.

Rick was certainly well equipped to help me figure out the financial meltdown inside David Smith & Co. He had just gone through an emergency surgery the week before for an obstructed bowel, however, so was at home recovering and in a lot of pain. His remarkable ability to rise up above his own pain and be of service was profoundly moving for me.

When Rick started wading into the utter chaos of David's business, he surfaced the question about whether I should accept the role of being the personal representative (PR) or executor of the estate, as I was named in the will. His question was whether it would be worth it to do all the work I would need to do in this role, or whether it would make more sense to just walk away from the mess with my suitcase and my cat and get on with my own life.

The latter idea was so antithetical to my nature. The thought of just leaving the ship to sink and take everyone's resources with it went against every cell in my body. And yet I also realized that this was not the time for blind heroics. I needed to take care of myself in this nightmare too. Clearly, David hadn't done that.

I had six weeks from the time of David's death to either accept or reject the role of PR. I asked Rick to help me assess the full extent of the business debt during that short window, and committed myself to performing the due diligence to understand as much of the reality of the situation as possible. While the abilities to listen for hidden messages and honor the mystical realms of life are key to Unfolding the Emergent, so is the ability to simultaneously be rigorous with assessing reality. It was essential that I investigate everything in David's hidden business world.

Although I had been an entrepreneur myself for many years, I had little experience with the wheeling and dealing of higher finance. This was David's forte—or at least I'd thought it was until now. He'd seemed to both love and hate the high-wire act of stretching way out past his means, borrowing money from various people and banks, and then snapping back in to make a payment right before the due date.

Rick and I met at the store many times with Chris, my new nephew-in-law and David's longtime assistant Carol. We walked through the 14,000-square-foot store—Indonesian prayer flags hanging, calming gamelan music playing in the background, and the scent of teak, and vetiver in the air—we made our way up the rickety stairs and into a windowless room with a cheap veneer boardroom table and a few broken office chairs around it.

It was like pulling back the curtain and seeing the scrawny old Wizard of Oz. All the charm and illusion was gone. What we saw was a business that was rotting from the inside out. David had been taking money from the company for years to fund his elaborate Vashon Sanctuary project, as well as a new project he was working on in Blitar, Indonesia—a beautiful, antique house that he was restoring with a good friend and planning to sell for millions of dollars. He used to say that everything he was pouring into the house made sense, as the money from the sale would fund our retirement. Although there was talk at first that I might see some of the financial return from the sale of that house, in the end his business partner just paid the taxes owed to the Javanese government and moved the house from Java to Bali. I never saw it finished.

Everything had clearly been hanging together through a combination of snake oil, illusion, and the loyalty of others to David's otherworldly brand and David himself. When he died, the spell was broken, and the reality was literally nauseating. More than once, I left the table in the dusty meeting room and made my way downstairs—past the furniture and customers—to the public bathroom. I would sometimes barely make it into a stall before vomiting. Holding on to the toilet bowl, my whole body shaking and my stomach heaving, I would wonder how I was going to get through this. When the wave had passed, I would wash out my mouth, take a deep breath, chew a piece of gum, head back upstairs—and make my path by walking.

Every day was like attending graduate business school, with only 30 percent of my intellectual capacity online. I met with lawyers, bookkeepers, accountants, those who were owed money, and his staff (in person in Seattle, by phone with his shop in Java), trying to put together all the pieces of this crumbling world so that I could see how to move forward.

One of the core practices of Unfolding the Emergent is letting go of old structures and ways of being in the world that no longer serve us. The limiting belief of the Crone archetype—*"I don't have enough knowledge, connections, or influence"*—was a constant chatter in my head. But I knew this old rap that had been passed to me through my parents, my teachers, and culture itself, and each time it surfaced I chose to tilt my awareness toward the liberating belief, *"I am an evolving source of wisdom, love, and power,"* as a mantra to remind myself that I didn't have to know it all yet, that I could focus on learning everything I could within the time frame I had and then make a decision. That I could trust my ability to listen deeply to myself and the signals life was giving me, and dynamically adjust and reset accordingly. I would Unfold the Emergent.

By the end of my six-week window, I had as much information as I could possibly get to make my decision about whether to take on the executor role or not. I understood now that the extent of David's debt far exceeded the only asset we had, which was our incredible estate—which I had, foolishly, put all of my savings from the sale of my waterfront home into, securing an additional five acres next to David's original twelve and doing various remodel projects to upgrade our home and the other antique buildings we had. So I had no financial cushion whatsoever to fall back on. I had trusted David implicitly. I had assumed, naively, that he would always have my best interests in mind.

The sobering reality I came to understand over those six weeks was that even if I were able to sell the house, I would personally get nothing because of the enormous debt David had to the banks and other people. The only chance I had of receiving any funds was if the court agreed to give me a "family support" award—a brilliant Washington State policy created to make sure that when one spouse leaves another that the former spouse is left with some funds, if they exist in the estate.

But I could only receive that award if the house was sold. And the amount given was established after the secured credit and the estate expenses were taken care of. So taking on the PR role was by no means a guarantee that I would receive anything at all at the end of the day.

On the other hand, if I didn't take on this role, everything would implode pretty quickly. The business would collapse, the bank would get the house and all its assets, and none of David's family or friends would see any of their money. David had a way of convincing people to loan him money, and it was staggering to see how much was owed to family and friends who had themselves risked their own retirement funds to support David's dreams.

It was one of the most important decisions I would make in my life. Everything was at stake. I was determined to use all of my ways of knowing—to walk the Way of the Mysterial Woman—to decide.

I had many conversations with family members and friends, seeking to hear different perspectives and feel how they resonated in my body. I spent time in meditation every morning and in long walks around the property, holding the question in my heart. I did a thorough, rational analysis, assessing the pros and cons. I consulted tarot cards, spoke with friends, watched my dreams, and looked for signs and signals.

I kept wanting to talk to David. I would spontaneously think, *I have to talk this through with David. He will know what to do.* Because he always had. No matter what challenges I faced in my own business or life, he'd always made me feel better when he calmly walked me through them.

But David wasn't here to help, and even when I reached out at the subtle level, there was only silence.

From all the work that I had done for many years, I knew to make space for everything I was feeling—for the anger, despair, sense of betrayal, terror, claustrophobia, wave upon wave of grief, and unexpected moments of sweet, loving connection; and for the horrifying recognition that my life the way I knew it, the future the way I imagined it, was slipping away and there was nothing that I could do about it.

I had a strong resistance to being labeled forever as a "widow" or to have my identity as a wife being connected in the same sentence with the word suicide. The cold, hard edges of language squeezed in on me—compressing and reducing my experience. Words like "suicide" and "widow" seem impossible to connect with who my beloved was and who I knew myself to be.

There would be no putting back together the pieces of my old life. Not yet. Not ever, really. First there would be more falling apart. And then, slowly, as I Unfolded the Emergent, a new life would form from the ashes of the old—and I would, if I was lucky, find myself standing on the ground of a new life.

For the moment, though, the reality of my situation was seeping in slowly, like an oil slick from a capsized tanker. You know that a brutal tragedy has occurred, but it isn't until you see the tar-covered birds flailing on the shore and the dead fish washing up that you can really take in the magnitude of what has happened.

This is as it should be. Your psyche knows what it can handle and when, and it doles it out to you accordingly, bit by bit over time. When a new wave of "what was so" came onto the shore of my awareness, it was my practice to steady my gaze and take in 2 percent more—even when I wanted to look the other way, to block it out, pretend it wasn't happening to me. The only place from which to Unfold the Emergent is firmly on the ground of the present moment.

My experience going for a blood draw to renew my thyroid medication was a rude awakening that brought me further into the new reality of my life. The middle-aged receptionist at the clinic barely looked up when she handed me the standard forms to fill out for my visit as she said, "Just fill these out quickly and we'll get you back for the blood draw."

Easy enough. The first text block asked for my name and I scribbled it in. But by the second box, I knew I was in trouble.

Date, it prompted—and as I wrote the numbers in, it suddenly sunk into some new place inside . . . David was dead. Even though I had found his body—stiff and empty of his beautiful essence, so completely lifeless—on that cold, rainy night in January, it wasn't until this moment when I had to connect with where I was in time that I reached this level of understanding that he was never coming back. That I would never again feel the soft skin of his beautiful hands touching me so tenderly, or find his little love notes tucked into my tea container, where he knew I would find them first thing in the morning. He was gone. And there was nothing, not a thing, I could do to bring him back.

I took a quick breath and forged on through the form.

The following box delivered the next dead bird on the shore—as hard to look at as the one before.

Address.

If I was lucky I would be selling our beautiful sanctuary on Vashon Island and looking for a place to rent in Seattle. I was going to be renting. After owning homes with Robert and then David for twenty years, how was that possible? The reality sank in—I would be saying goodbye to the seventeen acres of pristine land, our gorgeous home, the antique Indonesian buildings, the trees that had been there from the beginning and the hundreds that we'd planted, the standing stones from China that David had brought over for our rock garden, the Indonesian teahouse sitting in the wetlands where David had proposed to me, the exquisite gardens and ponds. I would walk through the gates and likely never again return to this place we had both loved with all our hearts.

My eyes blurry with tears, I did not know what to write. I remember the receptionist looking at me over the top of her bifocal glasses with what I took to be irritation that I was taking so long on the forms. Strangely, I did not judge her for the lack of compassion—how could she know what I had been through and what I was going through right then? To her I was just a woman taking too long on a form.

I quickly looked away and wrote my current address, because it was the only one I knew, and moved on to the next box, assuming the worst was over.

Marital Status.

My mind froze. I literally could not think of how to describe my status in a word. I was very much still married to a man who had run out of faith in himself and in his ability to handle the screeching tinnitus in his head and the imminent financial collapse of his company. He still loved me. I was his wife. *I am his wife*, I thought. And then the word "widow" washed up on the shore of my consciousness for the first time. I was a widow.

By now my throat was on lockdown as I tried to suppress the sobs that were just under the surface.

One more box to go.

Emergency Contact Number.

Well, my emergency contact was not here anymore! My emergency contact number was out of service. My beloved husband, who had committed to stand beside me in sickness and in health, had broken his promise. He would not be there if anything happened to me. I was alone. I managed to write the name of my dear friend Dianne, then fumbled through my phone to find her number.

The form was finally done. I was raw and shaky inside as I slid it back across the counter to the receptionist. This time she looked up at me as she took the clipboard. There was a kindness in her eyes as she said, "You can go on back now. It will be over soon."

I knew that was not true—that this pain would not be over any time soon. But I chose to take her simple words into my heart as a kind of fortune cookie message for the day.

———

Strangely, the experience at the doctor's office helped me to land in the reality of my situation and to face the difficult decision about whether to go forward as the executor of the estate or just walk away. I called Rick for one final conversation. My time was running out. I had exactly twenty-four hours left to make a decision.

"I know we don't have enough information yet to make a full assessment of things," I told Rick. "I know things look really bad. And I will take 100 percent responsibility for whatever decision I make. What I need to know from you is, do you think that there is at least a fifty-fifty chance that I could get through this and get people back some of their money?"

There was a long pause on the other end of the phone. And then Rick said, "Yes, I think there is. But I am still not suggesting you do it."

That was all I needed to hear. I had done my due diligence. I was not jumping into this role irresponsibly as a heroine coming to the rescue. By gathering information at all levels and trusting the unfolding process, I finally knew what I needed to do. On February 7, I wrote in my journal, *Important day with the lawyer. I chose to become the PR. We shall see what life has in store for me.*

I bowed my head and once again said, *YES—I will make my path by walking.*

Chapter 7:

Meta-Capacity—
Influencing System Resonance

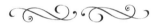

Engaging with the world using Influencing System Resonance means being a guiding influence to bring cultures, families, systems, and structures around you into harmony, beauty, and regenerative health. It means appreciating the contributions and competencies of the people around you and recognizing their profound creative potential—individually, and as a part of a collective.

When you are Influencing System Resonance, you see yourself as an integral part of the web of life and therefore recognize that you can positively impact the whole field by your actions. In essence, you become a tuning fork that helps organize complex and even fractured communities toward greater resonance.

When David took his life, he profoundly destabilized not only my world, but also the worlds of many who were connected to him—every person who was part of the complex system he was deeply embedded within. In order to Influence Systems Resonance after his death, I would need to first discover and embrace all the systems that were disrupted and then see if I could bring a kind of resonance into the discord. I would need to prune, nourish, dissolve, synthesize, and revise in order to increase the coherence, beauty, and potential of the overall traumatized ecosystem.

Ritual was one of the key tools I knew I would need to use as I worked to bring a subtle alignment and harmonization to the systems and structures around me.

Evolutionary Invitation:
Influencing System Resonance

Meditate on the words below and let them evoke your body, heart, mind, and soul. Imagine yourself as a woman on the edge of evolution Influencing System Resonance.

The seeds of the future are planted in
The ground of the present moment
In the very ecosystems where you are rooted

The solid foundation you have built and
The structures you are held by
Allow your sovereign nature to see out
Beyond yourself into the wider world

You know when to prune back, weed out,
Or reimagine the containers you need
For the well-being of the whole to emerge

You meet the structures of the world where they are
And take them somewhere they have never been
Willing to dissolve and shake things up
Knowing when to hold steady, move slowly, and wait

You are a tuning fork synchronizing
Everything around you into harmony
As the manifest and the unmanifest rejoice

Ritual Rite of Passage

I knew that I had an important role to play in bringing the larger systems connected to me and to David—family, friends, and community—into resonance if I could. Ritual was one of the potent tools I would use to heal myself and the larger pattern that had been torn asunder.

I had learned many years earlier that ritual process was one of the ways to help make sense of a world that made no sense to the conscious mind. "Without a ritual to contain and inform the wounds of life," Michael Meade wisely writes in his introduction to Mircea Eliade's *Rites and Symbols of Initiation*, "pain and suffering increase, yet meaningful change doesn't occur." I had already been using ritual for decades as a tool for transformation, and teaching women the power and wisdom of learning this ancient language in modern times. To get through the trauma of David's death personally, and to soothe the jangled nervous system of our community, ritual would be essential.

Ritual connects us instantly to the Mystery and, like archetypes themselves, serves as a vehicle to bridge between the unconscious and conscious worlds. It brings together the intuitive knowing from the body, the emotional feelings from the heart, the mental ideas and images from the head and our soulful selves. Ritual gives us powerful ways to heal ourselves and others, to acknowledge the important rites of passage in our lives, and to consciously celebrate sacred times of the year. It enables us to access and channel powerful archetypal and spiritual energies.

The need for ritual remains throughout our lives, and yet in our postmodern world we have very little training on how to consciously meet and nourish this need. Today, in fact, it has mostly been rejected as irrational, superstitious, or primitive. If we look at traditional or indigenous cultures we find a worldwide preoccupation with ritual action that cuts across all races, religions, and cultures. Globally, ritual was regularly used in all three of its functions—healing, rites of passage, and collective cohesion. These three aspects are the backbone of Influencing System Resonance, and I would use them all.

Throughout this book, I will walk you through many of the rituals I used to make my path by walking. I offer these so that you might use elements of them on your own journey and be encouraged to use this language of healing and integration. Don't be afraid to try something simple.

I began with the first ritual an hour after I found David's body. My women friends and I created a space in his study where we brought in the sacred in the midst of the horror. Helping David's spirit cross over to the other side in a surround of love on that dark, rainy, barren night was as much for me as it was for him.

People have often asked me how I got through those early days. What I can truly say is that it was one step at a time. Literally. Several days after he died, I began a ritual practice that I still use today and maybe will continue to use for the rest of my life. Each time I awoke from the dreamtime and came back into contact with the reality of my life, all I wanted to do was sink back into sleep and the other worlds that were not this one. It took everything I had in me to swing my legs over the edge of the bed, sit up, and put my feet on the floor—but when I did, I said my morning mantra: "I am deeply grateful to be alive and in this body and on this earth. May how I live my day be worthy of this precious incarnation."

I didn't always believe these words when I said them, but I cast them out ahead of me onto the blank page of the day and would do my best to live into them. In reading back through my daily WeMoon journal entries, I am struck by how often I said, "I do not know if I will get through this. Step by step, I guess." This morning commitment to one more day was all I needed—was all I could even contemplate.

The day after David died, my circle of women friends created a memorial altar to David in our Indonesian temple building—the remarkable antique teak building David had brought over piece by piece from Java. They set up a long altar table with photos of David, fresh flowers, a Buddha head, Japanese Zen singing bowls that could be rung, candles that could be lit, and prayers that could be written on small pieces of paper and hung on a big branch that draped over the table. There were meditation cushions in front of the altar where people could sit in silence, pray, meditate, and remember. Every morning, the space would be cleared of all the emotional energy people brought by burning fresh sage. The pungent smell lingered on, mixed with the teak, inviting anyone who entered into sacred space.

People came from the island and the city, needing somewhere to bring their grief and confusion, needing somewhere to pray and connect with David—a place to be with their shock and grief in community.

As I navigated the tsunami-devastated landscape of life without my beloved, my uncertain financial situation and the reality that I would be leaving our beautiful sanctuary, I would wander down there early in the mornings and later in the evenings—times when I thought I would not encounter anyone else—to sit by myself. Sometimes there would be someone there; when there was, there was a deep respect for our shared grief but we rarely spoke. We would just sit together and meditate; ring the singing bowl and leave. So many beautiful notes and prayers were left for David, and for me.

It was not until a month after his death that I closed this sanctuary down and we buried the prayers and blessings on the west side of the property, where they could go with the setting sun into the afterworld.

———

A week after David's suicide, Michael Meade offered to facilitate a ritual of release on the property where David had died. David's friend Brian no longer lived there full time and had not been on the property when David took his life in the hot tub. I will always wonder if perhaps David chose to die on this property because he knew his friend, who had a deep spiritual practice, could handle this horror. Or maybe he did not want me to find him in a bathtub in our house. Or maybe he knew that it would be very hard for me to sell the property if he died at home. Or maybe he was really only thinking of himself and wanted to die there—in a hot tub, outside in the fresh air with nature all around. Whichever it was, he had planned this departure carefully.

A small group of those of us close to the trauma gathered with Michael around where the hot tub had sat. It had already been dismantled, the bloody water of death drained from it. Michael led a ritual to release David's soul more fully from this last place where it had been embodied and to cleanse the earth the blood had poured into.

We all stood in a Circle. The stones that had been around the hot tub were gathered and stacked into cairns. Fresh water was poured over them as Michael called out an earth blessing that the Great Mother absorb David's wounds given to her through the blood and seal up the opening to make the land new again.

Directed to stand facing west, Michael led us in an African chant which we would come to use at many future rituals. He explained to us the ancient idea that song can carry what words alone fail to express and also that a song can transport us to the otherworld, where healing, restoration, and renewal can be found.

He chose a heart-opening chant that encouraged the soul in transition to move on and not look back. "Awé, Awé, Awé"—our voices rose together as we stretched our arms skyward. It felt good to sing, to be with friends, and I felt the world that had been thrown off its axis beginning to find a little bit of balance again. I could feel us coming into more resonance as a community. For a moment, a sense of sweet grace wafted through and soothed our souls.

This is what ritual and ceremony can do in the midst of chaos and disruption. A kind of system resonance comes into being, touching the sacred that is beyond the self.

———

Now that we had done our work to help release David's soul, the next step in Influencing System Resonance was to tend the shocked and grieving community and offer a ritual to help us integrate this cavernous loss. I had an inner knowing that if we could stabilize the core field of traumatized family and friends, we could all get through this together.

My life had been shattered like a ceramic vase on a cold stone floor, and there would be no putting the pieces back together again.

This was true for many others as well. Devastation and a sense of desolation hung over our landscape of loss. David was the charismatic eccentric everyone wanted to claim they knew, or claim as a good friend. This gentle, soulful David we all thought we knew so well was not someone who would have committed this violent act. The world was upside down.

Among the many who were especially devastated were Dianne and her husband, Richard, as they were our closest friends. Dianne had known David since they were twenty-six years old, when they lived across the hall from each other in an old Capitol Hill house that had been turned into six apartments. At the time David was doing about twenty-three hours of yoga a day and eating only sprouts, and Dianne was busy listening to loud music and dating as many men as she could. They were total opposites, and after moving out of their apartments they had lost touch with each other. Many years later, they'd reconnected, and since then Richard and David had become very close friends. Richard and Dianne had stood up with us in a beautiful Buddhist unity tea ceremony as part of our wedding.

I spoke to Dianne, an experienced psychotherapist, about my sense that we needed a group ritual to help us all move through the chaos and confusion and to "be with" everything that we were feeling. So often in situations like this everyone retreats into their own private world to try to heal and just get through the shame, grief, anger, and fear alone.

In our Mysterial work, a limiting belief of the Maiden archetype that our research revealed was, *"It is not safe to express myself fully."* During times of intense trauma, it is important for our healing that we have well-held containers in which we can move toward the liberating belief of, *"I am free to express my true nature."* We needed a ritual where each of us could express our pain authentically while being held within a supportive, loving community.

I invited Michael Meade to help us create and lead a ritual to that would allow us to process the embodied shock and trauma of David's suicide.

On January 12, with the new moon reflecting just exactly how dark this time was, about thirty-five people gathered at our house. My sister, Hannah, her husband, Brian, and my cousin Sarah had all just arrived from the East Coast to be with me. David's sister, Pam, and her son, Peter, were the brave ones from his family to show up. Many of our best friends were there.

My invitation had been clear—this would not be for everyone:

Our beloved David Smith's death has left us all in a state of shock and disbelief. There is much we have to release and process to reconcile the David whom we all knew and loved, and the David who took his life and left us all so suddenly.

I have asked Michael Meade and Dianne Grob to facilitate a group process to acknowledge and release the mixed emotions of grief, anger, confusion, fear, and emptiness around this tragic event. I am so deeply grateful for their wise and professional guidance.

This intimate time together is designed to help us to begin to move on without David, and to support him with our love as he transitions over to the other side.

Please know that you are in no way obligated to attend.

Note: This is by invitation only for a small group of family and friends. A memorial service will follow in a few months and will be an opportunity for all to join together in celebrating David's life.

―――――

It was a rainy afternoon, and the sky was heavy with clouds as people made the long trek down our winding driveway, onto a pathway through the woods, then across a stone bridge over a pond to finally arrive at our house. The mood was sober, and there was an undercurrent of anxiety; everyone was wondering what we were going to do and what it would mean for them. For many, it was the first time they had been to our house and the first time that I had seen them since David's death. Few words were spoken; mostly, we just shared teary hugs, barely holding the heavy weight of grief between us.

We had organized seating, from antique formal armchairs to zafus on the floor and everything in between, set up in the main open plan great hall living room. We had arranged it so that everyone was facing the stone fireplace at one end of the room. The rest of the walls were floor-to-ceiling glass doors with a broad view out over the landscape of the Olympic Peninsula. We had hung an ancient Tibetan brass bell—a gift David had long ago given to our neighbor and friend Marcus—from the ceiling rafter, and planned to ring it to start and end our time together. Cedar boughs were stacked in a pile by the roaring fire, ready for use in our ritual.

When we had all gathered, my shaman friend Antonia stood up with her rattles—two in each hand, her dark hair long and wild, her skirt swinging around her as she stepped in front of the roaring fire. As she and the rattles became one, she seemed to shapeshift into her shamanic self. She found the energetic frequency of David's suicide and rattled it into the room.

Something about that congruence immediately woke the whole field up and brought us together into the resonance I was hoping for.

As the intensity of the rattling rose to a fever pitch, I stood up with one of David's ancient Chinese bowls held gently in my hands. I had chosen a blue glazed one about six inches in diameter that was several hundred years old and already had a chip in it. It was important to me that it was an expensive, precious item and one that was already damaged. I walked up to the stone hearth and, with Antonia rattling all around me, I lifted the bowl high over my head and smashed it down on the cold stone hearth. No, there would be no putting back together again the pieces of our lives into the old form, after this shattering event.

The ritual had begun. The room was stunned into silence. My heart was pounding in my chest. Michael rose as I returned to my seat, and he spoke the first words of the night.

"In some indigenous cultures in Asia, when someone dies there is an ancient tradition of smashing plates, bowls, and glasses that belonged to the dead person. It is a way of honoring the dead and the reality that their leaving has shattered something forever."

Michael spoke slowly and deliberately, allowing the room to come to him.

"When someone leaves this earth in the sudden way that David did, it tears something in the fabric of all of our hearts. We do not understand why, and we wonder if there was something we might have done and didn't do to prevent it. Grief, shame, guilt, anger, fear—all these emotions are present." Michael paused for a moment and looked around the room. "Suzanne has asked you all here today to gather as a community on this dark day. To create a safe and sacred space where there is room for everything everyone is feeling. There is no right or wrong way to be a part of this evening. The fact that you are here means that something called to you and you can trust that."

Michael looked over at Dianne and invited her to offer a reading to set the tone for the sharing we would do.

Dianne slowly stood. She gazed around the room, softly making eye contact with me and the rest of our community, and then she drew in a deep breath and read these words by David Whyte aloud:

GROUND
To come to ground is to find a home in circumstances and to face the truth, no matter how difficult that truth may be; to come to ground is to begin the courageous conversation: to step into difficulty and by taking that first step, begin the movement through all difficulties to come, to find the support and foundation that has been beneath our feet all along; a place to step onto, a place on which to stand at last and a place from which to step.

Michael stood by the fireplace beside the pile of cedar boughs we had gathered beforehand. When Dianne finished her reading he said, "Another tradition, this one from some Native American tribes, is to lay cedar boughs on the fire as an offering to the spirits and an act of release as you let your loved one go."

He invited anyone who felt moved to do so to come forward, one at a time; say what they needed to say, or just stay in silence; and then lay the bough on the fire.

I held my breath, wondering if anyone would stand up in this vulnerable way—wondering if it was too much to ask.

But it didn't take long for the first person to jump up and come to the center of the room. It was Rob, who had found David's body.

A primal, guttural scream left his body as he stepped into the center of the room. After that raw emotion had ripped through his body, he slumped forward and wept. And when the wave of grief had rolled through he moved toward the fire and placed a cedar bough on the flames. We could see in his face and hear in his voice the brutal impact finding his friend dead had had on him.

Deborah, my friend and business partner who had been with me that first night, stood and said, "I did not ask for this. I did not want this. Your act has marked me forever. I will never forget everything that I saw that first night." She was angry, and I felt a rush of guilt and grief as I took in how my husband's chosen death had wounded her so deeply.

Others stood and spoke of their sense of betrayal and anger. Some stood to speak in quiet voices of their long journey of friendship with David and how much they would miss him.

Others spoke to how knowing David had positively changed their lives.

His sister bravely stood up and spoke to the loving relationship she'd had with him her whole life.

When Antonia, who had begun with the rattling, stood up, she had fire in her eyes and her body was shaking. The explosive words she spoke seemed to come not just from her but also from some global deep Feminine rage for all the harm that wounded men had inflicted on women.

"What the fuck is the matter with men!?" she cried. "Why do they lie and withhold and keep things from us? David, why didn't you tell us you were suffering so much? We could have helped you. You were not alone. You could have told us the truth."

Antonia's raw and almost transpersonal voice had opened space for outrage.

Stephen, a dear and longtime friend of David's, stood up at the back of the room and walked forward with his shoe in his hand. He unceremoniously hit the hanging gong with it.

"David—why didn't you talk to me? This is the sound I constantly hear in my own head." He hit the gong hard again. "I could have helped you. You could have learned to live with the sound."

With each smack of the shoe on the gong, Marcus, the person whose sacred bell it was, writhed on the floor as though he himself were being hit. It was a breathtaking moment; we could all feel the unbearable cacophony David had heard inside his head, and we could also feel the way in which the sacred had been violated by his suicide.

Dianne suddenly stood up and spoke her anger into the room. "This is exactly the split inside of David—between the sacred and the profane. And it is getting played out right now, right here. He left because he could not hold these two forces together—he could not stay in his body. He wanted only the bliss states and would not stay and face the discordant sounds in his head and the failures in his life."

This jarring process powerfully Influenced System Resonance. A ripple of understanding moved through the room, and although the interaction was extremely uncomfortable there was something congruent in feeling in our bodies the raw impact of his suicide in this way.

One by one, others stood and shared what was in their hearts. I waited for the signal inside to tell me when to speak. When it came, I stood up and walked into the center of the room, my body shaking.

Overwhelming grief and anger were a potent inner stew as I began, speaking directly to David, "David—why did you betray me? I saw you to your threshold—I stood with you and helped you complete your book. And now my threshold is coming—my book completing, my programs launching—and you left me at the door . . . you left Claire at the door . . . you left us all."

My voice softened. "I don't know how I will get through this without you. I can't even see the possibility of doing that. You were my dry ground and now I am in the suicide swamp of your making and trying to keep my head above water. I don't know how to hold both the you who left in this way and the you who I loved with all my heart. It will take time."

With tears streaming down my cheeks, I placed my cedar branch on the fire. My body was drained and limp as I took my seat.

———

Several others spoke before Michael led us through the final ritual. The night had crept in during the truth-telling, and now as he called us to all stand and face west, we were looking out of the glass doors to the dark horizon beyond.

My cousin Sarah had brought with her many little clay pinch pots the size of small sake cups that she had made. They were very raw, elemental, and misshapen, just like the moment we were in. We gave one to each person in the room, and into them we poured the last batch of David's kombucha, which had been brewing in the warm furnace room for weeks. It was one of his latest projects, and he'd tended the mother yeast like she was a child as he'd moved from one batch to the next. The kombucha, like the life we had known with David, would not be continuing on.

Holding up the cup in one hand and stretching his other arm out toward the heavens,

Michael led us all in song, a prayer for David, blessing him on his way. It was a song that we had already used when we cleansed the place where he had taken his life. We could sing it again now, our voices lifting together, because we had also presenced everything else we were feeling—"Awé, Awé, Awé . . ."

I knew for sure I was not going to do a spiritual bypass on this process. I was not going to transcend the embodied experiences of grief and anger and hurt. I also knew this was System Resonance in action—we were here, together, and ritual had helped us come into truth and harmony, even though the truth was painful for all of us to feel. We were not bypassing, we were all feeling it together.

David had not been able to do that. He had not been capable of staying in his body with his suffering. He had taught himself to go up and out to higher levels of consciousness when he was struggling—and ultimately this had led him to leave his body altogether, and to do so in isolation.

My path—the Way of the Mysterial Woman—was going to be down and in and with community.

Chapter 8:

Meta Capacity—

Embracing Paradox

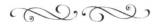

W hen we are in the midst of trauma or when life events require us to navigate a huge loss or change, the habitual mind will try to orient with dualistic thinking. This is good, this is bad; this is right, this is wrong. But the capacity we are all being asked to cultivate now goes beyond this limited frame and invites us to embrace a more complex and accurate reality. What if factors that initially seem like polar opposites could be held together long enough to allow something new to arise through their connection? As the late poet, author, and priest John O'Donohue said so well, "We learn to befriend our complexity and see the dance of opposition within us not as a negative or destructive thing but as an invitation to a creative adventure."

What if we could be open to the conversation between two apparent opposites in ourselves or with others in a way that allows us to be with uncertainty and resist the urge to quickly simplify, making it possible for something to arise from this complexity that is greater than the sum of its parts? This is what it means to Embrace Paradox.

From the very first night that I learned of David's suicide, I was required to hold many complex and seemingly contradictory factors together at the same time. I would need to be able to embrace all the dilemmas and paradoxes that were initially unsolvable in order for a creative outcome to arise through the differences. And as I embraced the many conflicting points of view, I walked a path that would lead me to the simplicity on the other side of complexity.

An Evolutionary Invitation:
Embracing Paradox

Read the words below and let them evoke your body, heart, mind and soul. Imagine yourself as a woman on the edge of evolution Embracing Paradox.

You let go of the struggle to hold all the complexity in balance
Expanding out in the spacious center that you have cultivated
Where there is room for it all

You do not rush to solve the unsolvable
Allowing the seeming opposites to dance together
Until they show you their alchemy

You can be happy while also standing in the river of sadness
Confident while also hosting the uncertainty of what will be
Trusting and afraid in equal measure
Willing to shake things up and honoring the structures

Holding your truth in one hand and another's in the other
You invite the multifaceted world to sit at your round table
Out beyond the diversity of worldviews
Lies a wide-open field of possibility

And it is here that you stretch out and
Welcome what is beyond paradox
Appearing like magic as a recognizable
Form in the clouds overhead

An Intruder Healing

In the days that followed our community ritual of release, there were many things I needed to sort through and figure out. It took determination to not quickly reduce everything to one pole or the other, especially when others were encouraging me to do just that. My capacity to Embrace Paradox was tested and cultivated again and again. Could I hold anger at David and compassion for his suffering, a desire to flee and a sense of responsibility, my own healing needs and the needs of the community, clarity and confusion, intuition and logical analysis, fear and courage, uncertainty and faith, all at once?

Six weeks after David's death, I had a profound opportunity to engage the capacity of Embracing Paradox. It was a tender day for me. I had just accepted the reality that I would sell our property and had begun to stage the house for sale. The monthly mortgage payments on our property were what had tipped the scales on David's fragile house of cards and sent everything cascading down. Our sanctuary had been his downfall—but it was also the only asset that had the possibility of providing some form of salvation in this bleak situation.

The real estate agent told me to remove anything that was unique or evocative of us so that potential new owners could see themselves living in the house. But I didn't want anyone to see themselves living in my house.

It was an excruciating process. All our personal items were to go—no books left randomly around the house by both of us avid readers, no colorful silk scarves draped over the antique Indonesian stand in the hallway or beautiful objects from faraway places we had visited. I had to dismantle the little altar in my office—put away the candle, sacred stones, photos of David, statues of Kuan Yin and the Buddha.

Many of our decorative objects were one-of-a-kind things that David had found in Asia. The act of gathering up the artifacts of my husband's years of searching around the globe for beauty and putting them into boxes was heartbreaking. It was one of the hardest things that I had done so far. With each object I put into a box, I faced the reality that David wasn't coming back and the finality of my departure from this life.

When it was done, the house looked as barren and hollow as I felt on the inside—empty, waiting for someone else to make it full again with joy and beauty.

As for me, I knew the emptiness inside was not going to be filled with lightness and happiness anytime soon.

Not quite two months into this nightmare, it was still so hard to believe how dramatically my life had changed since I'd heard the impossible words, "David is dead." The bottom had fallen out of my world; my beloved husband's sudden and chosen death had devastated me and all the outer structures of my life. It had brought me to my knees in a way that I could not imagine any other act doing. The fulfilling future that I had imagined ahead was simply gone. And there I was . . . on the edge of a new and unimaginable chasm.

Only a nanosecond earlier, David had been with me, cuddling me in bed; I had been his cherished wife and not this widow left hanging over the broken ledge of desolation—the one staring into the void, wondering what had happened. The sleepless, haggard one who had lost everything that mattered.

I was still very much testing the strength of my faith. Faith that my center would hold. Faith that in spite of this devastation, I did live in a friendly, benevolent universe. Faith that I would be able to travel across the rough ground of uncertainty. Faith that I could restore some kind of harmony and coherence to the chaotic world that was tumbling down around me. Faith in faith itself.

Daily I Embraced Paradox, balanced precariously on a thin razor's edge between holy terror on one side and steadfast hope on the other. It required all of me, all the time, to focus on not tumbling down into the dark void of despair.

On this Saturday, I stood in the middle of the depersonalized atrium of our living room and felt the desolation of my life. Everything had happened so fast. David, a good friend who was also our landscape designer, had offered to come by to assess all my valuable outdoor antique sculptures and stone vessels. I would need to sell them as well.

After a quiet cup of tea together in my mausoleum of a house, we walked down the winding path toward the driveway to begin our tour of the property. As we emerged from the trees, I looked up and to my horror saw smoke curling out of the chimney of our antique Indonesian guesthouse. It made no sense. Our property was very isolated. Nobody arrived here by mistake.

"Holy shit!" I yelled. "Where is that smoke coming from?"

The two of us ran toward the front door—which was, uncharacteristically, wide open. As we got closer to the house, I also began to hear music—*my music*—playing. We burst in through the door and into the room with the potbelly stove and were stopped in our tracks by a bizarre sight.

A scrawny young boy, who looked to be at most fourteen years old, was sitting on the sofa. As startled to see us as we were to see him, he sprang up as though to defend himself. I saw a confusion of different emotions run across his face. His eyes had that look of a wild animal caught in a headlight. He knew he shouldn't be there. This was the body of the vulnerable child. And then there was another layer—the bravado. Trying not to look afraid—to look like he could handle us if he needed to—he stood ready to pounce.

Sarah McLachlan's song "Angel" was blaring from my small iPod and speaker on the kitchen counter.

It was all so surreal—the music playing, the fire roaring, and this kid here in the middle of nowhere as though he were at home listening to music by the stove on a Saturday afternoon. On the coffee table in front of him were strewn items from my art studio in the building—an owl feather, a fan, an old journal, and a Chinese Calligraphy brush. And from David's desk drawer were his old passport, a driver's license, a timeworn leather wallet, and some rare antique Indonesian masks from a box I had packed up ready for moving.

In the split second it took to absorb all this, I felt a deep compassion for this lost child, a desire to scoop him up in a warm embrace like a loving mother and tell him everything would be okay. And I could also feel the outrage that someone was in my house and going through David's things. Both were true—Embracing Paradox.

"What do you think you are doing here? Who are you?" I said

as David turned off the music and crossed the room toward the sofa. "This is private property. How did you get in here? Who gave you permission to come in here?"

The kid kept looking back and forth between us and the door.

"The door was unlocked—I didn't think anyone lived here," he offered lamely, shifting his weight from one foot to the other as though he might make a run for it.

"So you just walked into someone else's house and decided to make a fire and put on music and go through their things?" David shouted.

"Yeah, well, it didn't look like anyone was here," the kid responded, as though that explained everything.

"How did you get here? Where did you come from?" I asked, incredulous.

"I came across the field past the strange building," he said, referring to our Indonesian Kudus temple building. "My dad is building a pizza oven for your neighbor Leah, and I'm helping him. They were talking about this place and I wanted to see where the dead man who killed himself lived."

His words hit me with a brutal blow to the gut; I could feel my body shaking in that PTSD kind of way that another shock after trauma activates. But the kid seemed oblivious to the insult of it all. Like a buzzard looking for a dead body, it all seemed to make sense to him.

"That dead man was my husband!" I spat out. "What is your name and who is your father?"

I asked this as though if I knew their names, the insanity of the situation would all make sense.

"Sean, and my dad is John," he offered, and I could see his shoulders begin to relax a bit.

"Okay, Sean. We are going next door to talk to your dad. Let's go."

I was glad to have a plan now and ready to get him off my property. But as he picked up his worn black bag and slung it over his shoulder, I saw the edge of a Bose speaker peeking out and my anger returned.

"Hey, what else have you got in the bag?" I asked. "Is that my speaker?"

Even after being caught breaking into my house, this kid was going to take a bag full of my things with him? I couldn't believe it.

He reluctantly began to pull stuff out of the bag as though he was sincerely disappointed that he wasn't going to get to keep these things. Out came the Bose speaker, as well as an antique metal pot, a 100-year-old Indonesian mask, and a clear resin amber pendant necklace with a scarab beetle inside that came from China.

"Do you realize we could call the police?" David threatened. "You are breaking and entering, *and* stealing?"

"Go ahead . . . I'm used to it," Sean said defiantly, as though this was almost what he was hoping would happen. But I knew that I could not face bringing police onto the property again so soon after David's death. The memory of them and the crime scene the night that I found his body were all too fresh.

With the bag emptied, we escorted Sean at a quick pace across our property and down the road to Leah's house. I was still shaking when we arrived there.

His father looked up from his tiling job on the pizza oven out back with confusion and Leah came out of her house as she saw us march past.

"Are you Sean's father?" I asked.

"Yes, I am. Did he get in trouble again?" He put down his tools, glowering at his son.

I told him the story of where I had found Sean, what he had done, and what he had said about David and the dead man. Leah, whom I had not seen since David's death, opened her mouth to say something and then closed it again, speechless.

"Sean is always getting into trouble," his father said to me. He turned and yelled at Sean, "I wondered where you had gone. I can't take you anywhere—you're just plain trouble." Then he looked at me again and said, "His twin brother would never have done this. He's a good kid. Their mother and me split up when the kids were young and she has mental problems. Sean is just like her—he makes it pure hell for everyone. He's a screwed up kid."

Even in my state of shock, something began to shift inside as I listened to Sean's father speaking. My outrage was dissolving into heartbreaking compassion. I could see the whole pattern here with his father. Sean had his head hung low, stringy blond hair over his eyes, and he was looking at his boots as he kicked into the dirt. I could feel his suffering in my bones—the shame and the hopelessness of it all. And I thought of David. Is this what he felt like before he left? This bleak sense of despair?

"I'm just a loser," Sean said. "Everywhere I go I cause trouble. You shouldn't have brought me with you. I'll never change. I shouldn't even be alive."

When Sean said these last words, something snapped inside me. I turned to face him full on and started speaking in a strong and steady stream.

"Yes you *should* be alive! Your life is precious—there is no one else like you here on earth." My voice rose in intensity as I continued. "You are not a loser—but what you did today was really stupid. You scared me and you hurt me by violating my home."

I was locked on to him now and truly didn't know whether I was speaking to Sean or to David or some weird amalgam of the two.

"And yes you can change—but you have to *want* to change. My husband David is not alive today because he gave up. So I don't accept your bullshit about not being alive. That is the easy way out. It is harder to stay and face the difficulties of life. But you can choose that. Right here. Right now. Today."

Once I had finished speaking, the energy drained out of me. It was as though I was transmitting some kind of life force into Sean, and when it was done I was done as well.

I looked over at David and said, "I need to go home now."

Grateful to have my good friend with me, we turned and walked in silence back to my guesthouse.

When we got there, I gathered up all the items strewn on the coffee table and I noticed the glint of something on the sofa where Sean had been sitting. My heart skipped a beat when I saw that it was a big carving knife from the kitchen drawer of our guest house. My first thought was that he had it to protect himself and that he could have hurt us. But my second thought moved me to tears. What if he was going to kill himself? Wasn't that what he had said over at

Leah's? What if he was following the trail of the dead man who killed himself? What if he fantasized about being famous like that guy?

I wanted to run next door and wrap this scrawny kid in my arms and tell him again that he was so precious and so loved. And I wanted to go back in time to the last morning that I saw David alive—sitting in the kitchen in the early morning light, beyond exhausted, his head hung low after another sleepless night due to the screeching of his tinnitus. I wanted to hold him in my arms and say, "You are the most precious person in the world to me. We will figure this out. We will. Don't give up. You're not beaten yet. Hold on."

It was too late for that now, but for Sean maybe a different path was possible.

As that thought crossed my mind, I looked down on the table and saw the scarab beetle necklace. I knew what I needed to do.

I grabbed it in my hand and ran outside to find David. I told him about the knife that I had discovered and how I wondered if Sean was planning to kill himself. "Will you do something for me?" I asked him. "I want to give Sean this necklace, but I don't have the strength to go back there right now. Will you go for me, and give him a message from me?"

When I'd told David what I wanted him to say, he looked at me as though I had lost my mind. "Are you kidding?" he said incredulously. "This is just going to reinforce him—that it pays to be a delinquent. He's going to see this as a reward."

Perhaps. It was a valid point, but I knew that I needed to do it anyway—for him and for me too. I needed to reach out to this wounded adolescent who was suffering. I wanted a chance to do that again. By reaching out to Sean that day, it was as if I was also reaching out to David on January 3.

This is exactly what Embracing Paradox looks and feels like—recognizing that there are multiple ways to see what is happening and, rather than making anything right or wrong, trusting the decisions that arise through staying with the complexity.

"Maybe," I told David "but I still want to do it. It is a huge favor I'm asking of you, and I will understand if you can't do it."

Seeing how serious I was about this, he reluctantly took the scarab necklace from me. "You are crazy," he said as he climbed into his car, "but I'll do it for you—not for the kid."

———

About ten minutes later, on his way home, David called to tell me what had happened. At first Sean didn't trust him and wouldn't take the necklace. But when David told him that he didn't agree with me—that this was not his idea and he would have called the police if it were him—Sean stuck out his hand.

"She is giving you this power necklace," David told him. "There is a very special scarab beetle inside. The young scarabs emerge from a ball of shit. Then, all of a sudden, wings emerge, and they fly away toward a new life. She wants this necklace to remind you that you are a good person inside—that shit happens, but you can get through it. Suzanne believes that you can change."

In the weeks that followed, I often wondered what had happened to Sean. A kid like that who also lived on a razor's edge between despair and hope . . . Was he even still alive?

And then, two months later, I received a small envelope in the mail addressed to Mrs. Smith—a name that I had never taken as David's wife. Inside was a handwritten note done in the kind of cursive writing that you learn to do in fourth grade—big, loopy letters exactly fitting between the lines. It was heartbreaking to imagine how much time had been taken to write this note so earnestly—spelling, grammar mistakes and all.

Dear Mrs. Smith,

I am so sorry for braking into your house and steeling your things.

If there is any projects that my Dad and me can do for you around your house I would like to help.

Sincerely, Sean

He was alive! The relief I felt knowing this surprised me, and it confirmed what I was coming to know to be true: You make your path by walking—one step at a time. If I could be compassionate one more time than I was judgmental, have faith one more time than I was fearful, be loving one more time than I was withholding, forgiving one more time than I was resenting, then maybe I would find the hard and holy trail of my own becoming in this dark night. And then maybe this would be a small light for a wounded boy lost in the wilderness and he would slowly see, there beneath his feet, the tracks of a new life.

Chapter 9:

Meta-Capacity—

Multi-Dimensional Knowing

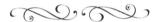

We are navigating a rapidly changing world, just as the planetary threats and stakes seem higher than ever. Simultaneously, we are seeing the limitations of our old ways of thinking and old beliefs as we try to manage these changes—which is why it didn't surprise me when I saw women who had completed the deep work of our Mysterial Woman programs giving birth to a much more expansive navigation system, which I call Multi-Dimensional Knowing.

As we differentiate from the patriarchal structures that keep us doubting and even silencing the truth of our inner experience, our deeper feelings and body wisdom, we begin to see that cultivating a Multi-Dimensional Knowing is crucial. It is the ability to engage ways of knowing and seeing from the rational and analytical through to the mystical realms of night dreams and synchronicities, consulting Tarot cards and intuitives. It means hearing how a bird's cry seemingly aligns with and reinforces our inner thoughts, or watching the clouds darken and considering, *Why now?* It means noticing what our heart tells us in the moment, paying attention to the wind shifting or a random comment by a stranger passing by, and letting these all into our frame of knowing as valid information, equal to the past assumptions, logic-sifting, and lengthy googling for answers.

There were many important and high-stakes decisions to be made in the first few months following David's death, and in order to make them I would need to draw on all the ways of knowing that I had cultivated through the decades. I would need my capacity for logical and rational analysis. I would need my embodied intuition and the information that would come to me through my feelings. I would need to watch my dreams and be alert to the signs and synchronicities pointing me in certain directions. I would need to watch the cycles of the moon and the planetary influences in order to align with the larger patterns beyond myself. And I would also need to call on my capacity for "not knowing" and being with the Mystery as a place of possibility and power.

An Evolutionary Invitation:
Multi-Dimensional Knowing

Read the words below and let them evoke your body, heart,
mind, and soul. Imagine yourself as a woman on the edge of
evolution expressing Multi-Dimensional Knowing.

The inner well of silence is full with water of a wise life
And you drink daily from this source
Your body waits for the slow pulse of knowing to
Send its signal from the depths
And holds its wisdom without needing to understand

Your heartstrings wait to be plucked
And then you ride the song wave until it offers its music
Your wise mind joins in
Not held hostage by past stories
Reflection, analysis, logic sifting, and sorting
The voice of your soul, dowsing for the path
Guides you to the center

Not knowing is your gateway into another world of insight
And you stand there wide open to the signs and synchronicities
Directing you forward

You are the wisdom seeker and the truth keeper
Parting the veil for a glimpse of the new world
Living into the questions that you were born to answer

Calling in Guidance

When someone you love is ripped out of your life suddenly, nothing makes sense anymore. You know intellectually that they are gone but there is a constant nagging sense that they are about to come back. After David died, I found that I had an intense and persistent longing to speak to him just one more time. I wanted to say the things that hadn't been said yet. There are so many things that you just hold out saying because you think you have years to say them. I wanted to say that I would be with him no matter what happened. I wanted to feel his warm, thin body curled up behind me, letting me know that we would get through this horror together. My limbic longing for him was excruciating—like a limb that has been amputated and you keep reaching with it anyway.

In the midst of all the confusion after he died and all the difficult decisions I had to make, my mind kept instinctively turning toward David to help me figure it out: *What do I do with your business? How do I respond to the Bank of America calling with increasingly threatening calls to foreclose on our home? Should I take on the PR role for your estate or just walk away from it all? How much should I sell that Guy Anderson painting for? Tell me again how much you bought this ancient stone urn for in Bali?* I felt a kind of desperation to reach him.

From all the reading that I had done before his death, I understood that souls need time to go through the difficult journey from this dimension to the other. I had also read that those who take their own lives often require a longer time to move through to a place of peace and light and have the ability to connect with their loved ones again. Even if it didn't always lead me to comfortable or expected places, my natural ability to trust and cultivate Multi-Dimensional Knowing became the anchor of my inner navigating system in the months and years to come.

Since Kim, the shaman who had done the ritual with me on the night of his death, had said that David had crossed over to the other side quickly, I only waited a few months before contacting various psychics whom I hoped would have the ability to connect with him. Finally, I got in to see a woman but she told me that he wasn't quite ready to speak with me yet—that he was still healing and going through his transition. I told her that if I knew he would be with me on the other side as a guide, I thought I could get through this. It would be like when he was in Indonesia for extended times and we would communicate by fax and phone. I wanted him to tell me about everything he had found on the other side, tell me he loved me, was sorry he left in the way that he did and reassure me that I would be okay.

She told me that he was still covered with red—like red paint or red blood, like a man who was marked—and he was walking around with enormous shame. Without mincing words, she said, "He is not your soul guide. He is literally not capable of being that for you, and you need to let him go. He is still in his own process and fighting with his team, saying that he wants to return to be reborn in a monastery." His team, meanwhile, was apparently trying to convince him that he needed to choose a life where he could heal the karma caused by his most recent life. Hearing this, I had an image of a very civilized conversation between a team of parents and a wayward teen, the parents trying to steer him back toward the direction of his growth when all he wanted to do after his egregious actions was go home and bliss out.

This was not what I wanted to hear. I wanted to hear that yes, he was my beloved, and he was right there on the other side trying to say *I'm sorry.* That he just couldn't let go and make his journey to the other realm because he was so heartbroken about what he had done. That he would stay and help me get through everything before going on to the land of bliss.

But no. And this was a hard thing to hear from a random stranger, but it rang true. David had not been able to stay with me through this life; why was I thinking that he would all of a sudden start showing up in the next?

When I closed the door to him that afternoon and stopped my frantic reaching upward, I landed hard down here on the earth. I was on my own. I felt so many of my problems and challenges needed

David's input. He'd always known how to figure out what to do next. But now it was up to me.

———

Another well-known local psychic I visited claimed to have contacted him, but I did not feel anything or believe what she was saying to me. She had known David and seemed to have her own personal agenda about him and his spiritual bypass. She told me that he was standing at the end of the massage table with an armful of white lilies for me. (That was somewhat synchronous, as we both loved lilies and often filled our house with their scent.) But she also reported that David wanted to tell me that he now realized that I was the old soul and that he wasn't even as spiritually awake as my baby toe.

This all made me very angry. Angry at the psychic, at David, at myself. It was true that everyone seemed to project onto David that he was someone with a deep spiritual wisdom. And it was true that he had not been able to translate those states of being into the material world and face into the dismantling of his dreams. It was also true that I, not he, was the one living through this nightmare with courage and grace and compassion. But I was not quite ready yet to fully accept that mantle.

———

As I was not having much luck with psychics, I began to go to bed every night with a prayer that David would come to me in my dreams. I had read that souls were often able to communicate with their loved ones through the dreamtime—so, night after night, I kept my dream journal at the ready. But nothing. He did not come.

Finally, the truth of this Multi-Dimensional research sank in. I was not going on this healing journey with David—I was going on it alone. I would make my path by walking, and it was time for me to surrender more fully into all the feelings of this enormous loss.

Right when I needed it, Sharleen offered her cottage on Maui as my sanctuary for this surrender and I invited Antonia to go with me. In the aftermath of David's death, Antonia and I had become close friends—accelerating what might have taken many months of openness and trust to cultivate. As a therapist and shaman who had tumbled into the darkness with me, I could not have asked for a better ally on this descent into my deepest feelings. She and I went together to rest in the energy of Mother Maui, with her warm breath and soothing waters.

I had been living in the strange liminal place that you go to when grief rips the doors off of your house of being and the wild winds of trauma blow through your inner sanctuary. Everything is upside down and you just want some shred of normal. Once we arrived on the island, I suggested to Antonia that we go shopping—because we absolutely had to have a teapot. And not just *any* teapot but a very special kind, with a strainer.

Antonia was very patient with me as we traipsed from Costco to Target to Macy's, searching. This was my way to try to feel normal and go to the places that other people who had not lost everything went to. I wanted to blend with the regular world for a few hours.

Once I had my teapot and we had settled into Sharleen's place, I finally let myself really be with the enormous grief, anger, and fear, and the thaw began. Ever since David's death, I had been so focused on taking care of all that had to be organized—preparing our house for sale, trying to find buyers for our huge and expensive paintings, and figuring out what to do with his business and mine, to name just a few of my tasks—that I had had little time to let myself unravel. Until this moment, it had been about getting through the daily onslaught of decisions and uncertainty while managing the waves of shock, anger, fear, and grief that were reverberating through my system. But now, with time to breathe, it began—a deep inner reckoning with the fact that David's decision to take his life had totally devastated mine. It was raw and real, and I just kept turning toward the truth and the hard feelings—as much as I could face in any one moment.

I had read about the Haleakalā volcanic crater, which was not far from where we were staying in Makawao, and I knew that this was where I needed to go first. The tallest peak of Haleakalā ("House of the sun") is 10,023 feet high, and from the summit you look down into a massive depression with steep walls and an interior that, aside from its scattering of volcanic cones, is mostly barren. The whole area is a sacred space for native Hawaiians, who visit the mountain to perform ancient rituals, including burial of the dead. It was the perfect place for me to take my grief and anger and for us to do a ritual of release.

It was late in the afternoon and there were few others in the park when Antonia and I arrived. As we set off down the trail, we naturally fell into a deep silence, each of us finding our own pace and place on the path. For the first time since David died, I felt an outer landscape matching my inner world. It was a hot, rugged, and unforgiving territory, with blood-red rocks and low scrub bushes and long, expansive views. Various low, foggy cloud formations drifted in and out of the canyon, sometimes totally obscuring the view and other times opening and giving us a glimpse way down into the basin of the crater.

Using the tuning fork of my Multi-Dimensional listening, I seemed to hear the spirit of Haleakalā saying, "Yes, you can give me everything you've got. I will meet you wherever you need to go."

And so I raged against the dark night that I had been thrown into. I called out for David, demanding to know how he could do this to me. How could he throw me into this hell? How could he leave me alone in this desolation? How could he abandon our marriage commitment, made only three years earlier, to love and stay present with one another—a commitment we had sanctified in our vows and inscribed on the inside of our wedding rings in the words of T.S. Eliot?

> *We must be still and still moving*
> *Into another intensity*
> *For a further union, a deeper communion.*

I sobbed uncontrollably, my body bent over the rocks, feeling no need to make it pretty or worry about how anyone else might be feeling. In great, heaving waves, I grieved the loss of my beloved partner, the loss of a future with him. I grieved the loss of my innocence. I let my body shake with fear for my future. There was no obvious way out of this mess for me. I could not see it. I gave the volcano everything I had . . . until I was truly empty.

Eventually, Antonia and I found each other farther down in the crater, and we sat together in silence on a big outcropping of red rock. I had found small stones that represented different beliefs, feelings, and outerworldly things that I needed to let go of now. One stone for the me who had an amazing present and possible future with David; another for the home and island community that I would need to leave; one for the belief that something like this could never happen to me; another for David's shame, and mine. One by one, I spoke these truths and threw the stones off the ledge and let them fall far below.

When I was done, we gave thanks and an offering to the spirit of Haleakalā and turned to walk back up the trail.

We were both emotionally drained as we started the walk up. We had not realized how far down we had gone and had not taken into account the high altitude. It felt like I was walking in lead boots; each step requiring enormous effort. The sun was already sinking low, and we were feeling the pressure to get out of the crater before the cold and dark of night descended.

It took two hours to get back up a trail that had only taken thirty minutes to descend. It was a powerful metaphor. I kept saying to myself, *One more step . . . that is all that you need to do.* I did not know then that this would become the metaphor, anchored in my body through this experience, that I would live into for the next many years.

When everything falls apart, there is only what is directly in front of you, and that one step is what you need to take and it is enough. In traumatic situations, the reptilian brain tries to recruit the prefrontal lobe to get safe again with stories from the past or fearful thoughts about the future. It is a practice to stay present in your body and use your focused mind to navigate the present rather than ruminate over the future or the past.

We make our path by walking, by opening to many different dimensions of knowing as we move over the brutal landscape of loss.

⁓

The next day, after the tough and cathartic struggle out of Haleakalā crater the day before, Antonia and I were ready to surrender to Mother Maui's softer side in the ocean. Once the morning sun began to heat up we packed our swimsuits, beach chairs, towels, and sun creams and set off for the beach.

The steady crash of the surf and the smell of the sea were soothing to my raw nerves and shattered heart. As I looked out just over the first swell of waves I saw a cluster of people on paddle boards all gathered around what appeared to be leaping dolphins.

"Oh my God, Antonia, I think there are dolphins out there!" I shouted.

She turned and saw what I saw, and then the two of us ran full out into the sea. It was one of our deepest desires to swim with the dolphins while in Maui but we'd had no real hope of experiencing such a thing. Usually they are way out beyond the reefs; they rarely come close to shore, and are even less likely to do so in areas where people are swimming.

It became obvious quite quickly that they were way too far out for us to get to them without paddle boards, but we were both beaming ear to ear just to be in the same waters. I dove down toward the sand and made a call like a whale, thanking them for their presence. Just knowing they were swimming nearby made my heart almost happy.

But then the most extraordinary thing happened. As I bobbed, treading water in the moving sea, I suddenly saw at least ten dorsal fins swimming directly toward me from farther out, and they were moving fast. I couldn't believe it. Suddenly they were all around me—moving with speed and purpose. I was giddy with the energy of it all. They did two passes around me, and then they took off and headed out to the wide-open sea, taking some of the weight of my grief with them.

In that moment, for the first time in two months, I felt my heart crack open to feelings of joy and love. Later when I returned to shore, I would learn that Antonia had experienced the same thing. Others who were swimming nearby told us they had watched the dolphins swimming around the two of us and marveled at the miracle of it all.

I had heard that dolphins have this ability to attune to your heart and heal wounds by their very presence. In my Multi-Dimensional Knowing, I feel sure that they came to us—maybe called by the spirit of Haleakalā—to gift us with their loving energy. Although there would be many dark days ahead, the burst of unequivocal joy, happiness, and pure love that streamed through my body in the presence of those dolphins was a vital opening that told me the spark of my life had not totally gone out—and that with time and patience, it would one day be possible to find happiness again.

~———

With Antonia's shamanic guidance it was time, after all the release and healing, to enter into a despacho prayer ritual as another way to open my Multi-Dimensional Knowing and connect with other levels of reality. A despacho, from a South American indigenous tradition, is a prayer bundle or offering—an expression of gratitude to heal physical and emotional ailments of any kind, to restore balance or harmony where it is off, and to make specific requests of the spirit world.

The power behind despachos, and the most important ingredient in the process, is intent. As with any ritual, having a special connection with each component of the despacho is what allows our feeling center to open wide.

Antonia had brought elements for the ritual. On the day we performed it, we also went out into the garden to collect flowers and fruit that we would need. She spread out a large piece of paper on the table and we slowly filled it with flower petals, sand, banana leaves, tobacco, fruit, and rice. With every offering we added to the paper, we blew a prayer into it. It was a sacred ceremony of hope and intention. When the despacho was complete, Antonia wrapped it up like a special package with bold red string; then she rang small shamanic bells around it, over it, and over me to sanctify and seal my prayers.

Having created the despacho, the next step was to offer it to the forces of nature. You can do this by either burying it (for slow, steady results), burning it (for quicker transformation), or feeding it to the running waters ceremonially. We decided on water, and we knew exactly where we needed to go: Waimoku Falls, a sacred Feminine, 400-foot-tall waterfall in a lush tropical rainforest on the easternmost point of Maui.

———

The hike in to Waimoku Falls was not easy, and as we moved through many different landscapes it became clear that Antonia and I moved at different paces, as we had in the volcano. I knew that I had to find my own rhythm to this next sacred ritual. And my pace was running.

After all the constriction of the previous two months, it felt so good to stretch out my legs and run free through the twisting trail, over tree roots, around an ancient banyan tree, under low-hanging branches, past smaller waterfalls, over creeks, and, suddenly and surprisingly, into a bamboo forest.

The bamboo was so out of context to everything else I had been running through that I was stopped in my tracks. Enormous green stalks stretched in every direction, completely blocking out the sun. There was no one else around. As the wind blew through, the eerie creaks and moans of the bamboo in the wind became a kind of symphony of whispers, chimes, clunks, and shuffles. Using Multi-Dimensional Knowing, I tuned my listening toward the bamboo.

It felt like nature's initiatory threshold, asking me to slow down and change my state completely before being swept into the awaiting power and beauty of the Waimoku Falls. And it was awesome—sheets of water cascading down over 400 feet of rock, moss, and outcroppings into a watery amphitheater below.

I sat quiet at the base of this rushing water as it pounded into the pool. It felt cleansing to let the sound explode through my body and feel the water spray on my face. When Antonia arrived, we looked for a place to leave our despacho—a spot where the water element would work its wonders over time, carrying my prayers to the Great Mother. We found a little crevice on the rock wall to one side and, saying our prayers, we tucked it into the stone.

I felt lighter after this ritual. Like some parched, dry place inside me had been watered.

———

After ten days in a kind of time-out-of-time space on Maui, I knew I had to return to my estate executor role and the hard reality of what I had left to do. But my time on the island had brought some color back into my gray world. My eyes and heart had been fed by the rich greens of the palm trees and sugar cane, the brilliant turquoise of the ocean, the bright pinks and purples of the flowers, the deep blue of the sky itself, and the warmth of the sun. I had swum with dolphins and been blessed by their joy; I had taken in the strength of the humpback whales; I had been reminded by the bamboo forest of how important it is to be rooted and flexible at the same time; I had given the weight of my burdens to Pele in the Haleakalā Volcano; I had let the ocean hold and rock me into a knowing that I was part of a vast and interconnected oneness that was love. It had been deeply healing, and I would draw from this Yin well many times in the days ahead.

I still had to sell the house, close down David's business, identify all the creditors that were owed money, organize his memorial, do an inventory and pricing of all the antique furniture and stone objects I was selling, feed the vultures at the Bank of America who were circling around our home, and work with my business partners to relaunch the program that was meant to begin six days after David died.

But more excruciating than considering all of these things on my to-do list was realizing that when I arrived back on Vashon I would be the wife of the dead man who committed suicide. It was a slippery slope from that thought to all the attached anxieties, and I would have to keep myself upright. I knew that wherever I went, people would look at me with that combination of sorrow, compassion, and confusion that I had come to recognize. David's act had cast us all into a very uncertain world, and none of us knew the language there. Should we pretend we didn't see each other or say hello; should we make eye contact or look at the ground?

Suicide is such a toxic stew. People want to be compassionate but don't know what to say, and perhaps don't want to get too close to the suicide nuclear dump site, for fear that they might get contaminated. I imagined others wondering what made him do it and why I hadn't been able to stop him and what was I going to do now.

While there were many things I was uncertain about, however, I was crystal clear that I would not be sucked down into the suicide swamp of shame. I knew it to be a powerful force—like the spinning centrifugal force a big boat creates when it sinks, pulling everything within miles around into its descent.

David himself must have been awash in shame before he took his life. The extraordinary world that he had built was about to come tumbling down even as he completed a book that spoke of the possibility and marvels of awakening into the world.

There were so many resources that would have been available to help him if he had been able to reach out beyond his pain to other dimensions of support. But he hadn't.

I would not hide the reality of his death. It was not me who'd chosen to die by suicide, it was David. And just as much as he'd had the right to choose how he left this world, I had a right to choose how I would live in it.

However it was that I would make my way forward, one thing I knew for sure was that using Muti-Dimensional Knowing to do it was my best chance to arrive in a new world beyond the desolation of the one I was leaving behind.

Chapter 10:

Meta-Capacity—

Tending the Field

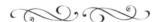

Tending the Field lifts us out of the limited mindset that we are alone in the world and brings us into the intricate pattern that connects us to all beings at all levels, as well as to our beautiful blue planet. We are not alone. During a worldwide pandemic, destabilized governments, a climate crisis, and social upheavals, we need to know how to tune in to all levels of existence—the gross (material), the subtle (emotional, imaginal, energetic), and the causal (Great Mystery, spiritual).

These extraordinary times are calling us to something new. The old mechanistic worldview had us convinced that we were on our own and that tending to ourselves and our tribe was all that mattered. The capacity of Tending the Field allows us to view and respond to our rapidly evolving world more expansively and at the same time more precisely, even in the midst of challenges. This capacity also asks us to keep our own instruments well tuned so that we can sustainably become wise stewards in the world.

There were so many possible ways that the tragedy of David's death could unfold for me and others close to him. I was very clear that in order to achieve the best possible outcome, I would need to attune to the symphony of emotions, concerns, expectations, and hopes of those who had been most profoundly impacted by the trauma. I would also need to take care of the subtle energetic patterns that had rippled into other dimensions of being and the land itself from his sudden death. I knew how to create a deep well of shared meaning; now I needed to keep the water flowing with gratitude and appreciation for all those who were bringing offerings. I needed to hold steady in the chaos and create the right enabling conditions for a new order to emerge.

An Evolutionary Invitation: Tending the Field

Read the words below and let them evoke your body, heart, mind, and soul. Imagine yourself as a woman on the edge of evolution Tending the Field.

Vibrating from the center
Your awareness ripples out in all directions,
In all dimensions,
Touching every level

You are the conductor of a great collective symphony
Receiving all that is vibrating in the present moment
Without judgment

Cueing in the subtle notes and the most brash
Knowing which ones to silence, to harmonize, to take center stage
The orchestra itself larger than any one instrument

You tend the heat of conflict as an alchemical
Fire turning lead into gold,
The sweet waters of appreciation harmonizing the differences

Your whole being resonates with the music of the field
As you tune it toward the possible

Letting Go

When I returned from Maui, the next most pressing and daunting task was to find a buyer for our unique property with all of its antique buildings, stones, water features, and incredible gardens. I would need to Tend the Field wisely in order to pull this off, tuning in to all the factors at all dimensions of reality without getting overwhelmed or freaking out.

I knew that all the trees and buildings and stones on the property were connected to David's energy. I needed to release him from that stewardship and take the mantle of care onto myself before I could open the energy up for the house to sell.

David's financial nightmare was now mine as well. But I was ill-equipped to handle it. Debt had never been easy for me—and his debt was so overwhelming that it was clear I would need to sell the property quickly to avoid having it taken from me by the bank. If that happened, all the money that was owed to his friends and family would likely never get paid, and I couldn't let that happen. The only asset I had to scale his mountain of debt was our estate.

I called together some of my closest friends who understood the importance of working with subtle realms of energy to help me with this ritual. David's old driver's license—the one that had emerged during Sean's unexpected visit—was the symbol I chose to use to release his stewardship of the land. I tied it to a stone with a cord so that it would be heavy enough to sink in the water.

In silence, we walked into the wetlands at the east end of the property to my favorite place—the Moon Viewing Teahouse, as we called it. David had built it for me a few years after I moved to the property. On a hot summer afternoon, he'd told me that he wanted me to see somewhere special he had found—a place he thought I would love because it was so Feminine and the sound of birds were everywhere. He held my hand and guided me through the wetlands, which in summer were bone dry, until we came to a clearing. We sat down and it was so beautiful, quiet, and soft in there. The rest of our property was so open, the views expansive and bold. This place was more like me . . . cozy and contained.

"I am going to build you a little teahouse here," he said. "I can already picture it."

And sure enough, within two years the antique, gazebo-like structure had arrived in pieces in a container, along with the ancient stone rollers from China that would become the stepping stones through the winter wetlands. And with the help of Peter, a Polish stonemason, it was complete before long. It was a magical place and we spent many sweet moments there, listening to the birds or in the spring to the frogs croaking voices lifting together in their mating chorus.

But the most special time there was when he proposed to me.

———

David knew that I loved romantic things and especially loved his words and invitations in writing. On August 14 (the Buddha's day of enlightenment and a super full moon) we went to town to see a movie—*Mama Mia* about love later in life and a crazy wedding on a Greek island. We did not know what the film was about when we went, but it turned out to be a quite perfect choice.

David had arranged for our neighbor Brian (the same person whose hot tub we later found David in) to light candles all the way down the stone path to the teahouse while we were away. When we arrived home, David suggested that we stroll around the property on this full moon night. This was not unusual, as we often did this together in the evenings. And of course we would go to the Moon Viewing teahouse.

As we turned off of the driveway and onto the stone path, David suggested that I go first. I could see the candles twinkling on the stones ahead—it was totally enchanting.

When I stepped up into the open-sided teahouse, there on a ten-foot banner, in the most beautiful calligraphy, was written . . .

Suzanne, will you marry me?

I burst into tears. I knew how much it had taken David to get to this point. He'd never thought he would marry, and I knew that it was a brave step forward to extend this invitation from his heart. I wonder sometimes now whether part of his reservation to get married came from his ambivalence about being here on earth.

But on this night he stepped farther into the world and into a commitment to love. He read me a letter that he had written to my father the week before, telling him that he was planning to ask me to marry him—and it was quintessential David. So well-written. He spoke of his love for me and how he hoped to bring me great happiness. And he told my father that he would take care of me, love me, and honor me.

My father died of prostate cancer two years after our marriage and so, thankfully, was spared the pain of seeing David break the promise he'd made to him and to me.

On this night, weeks after David's death, I stood on the same platform where he had proposed all those years earlier, holding the rock with his driver's license in my hand, and said, "David, you have been the caretaker of this beautiful property for many years. You named it Pusaka, which means 'place of spirit' in Indonesian. Your vision and heart and soul are poured into this place. You have chosen to leave this world, and now you must let go of your role as steward of this land."

We all said together the ancient Hawaiian Ho'oponopono Prayer for Forgiveness, Healing, and Making Things Right.

I am sorry,
Please forgive me.
Thank you
I love you.

"As I release this stone into the pond," I continued, "I also release you, David, as the guardian of this property." I could feel the words being sourced from deep within me—yet another level of letting go of my beloved partner—as I threw the stone into the pond and rang a singing bowl to mark the act.

I stood tall on the platform and claimed my new role. I was now managing the energy of this place. "I accept the mantle of stewardship of this land—of all the plants, stones, animals, and being at all levels."

With this declaration, the property came into my hands and, most importantly, into my heart. It was now my job to Tend the Field. I would listen to what the land needed from me to let it go, and I would invite in the next steward of this sanctuary whose destiny it was to be here.

My friends and I walked all around the perimeter of our seventeen acres and at various points we stopped and said the Ho'oponopono Prayer and I rang the singing bowl. I gathered up the Kudus House, the spring-fed pond with its marsh grasses and dragonflies, the territorial view of the sweep of the Shinglemill Creek valley below, the Japanese maple grove that we had planted only a few years earlier, the rare Dawn Redwood trees that turned to burnt amber in fall, the wide expanse of the western horizon looking out over Puget Sound, Kitsap county and the Olympic Mountains, the layered, rolling hills—so similar to Balinese terraced rice paddies—that surrounded the Kudus House, all the exotic plants and landscaping, the Chinese Indonesian antique house, where we'd held so many musical and Buddhist events, the enormous standing stones David had picked out one by one in China and placed carefully in his Japanese garden surrounding the Kudus House.

We finished at our home and I gathered that up too, standing in the great hall living room with the enormous glass doors on all sides. The singing bowl echoed for a long time as we all stood there, silent and somber, and the weight of the burden of responsibility that was now mine pressed down on my small shoulders.

I had two months at the most to find a buyer for this extraordinary place.

———

In Tending the Field, along with selling the house, I also needed to figure out what to do with David Smith & Co. David had tied the two together in what had turned out to be a very unholy alliance, and now I would need to disentangle them from one another. The business was in freefall already; if David were there, he would have been juggling funds from one loan to another in a kind of wild circus act. I certainly could not duplicate such a thing, so I had to find my own way.

With no one to run the store, and the burden of debt it carried an unattractive prospect for anyone, it was clear that we would need to shut everything down with a fire sale–like auction. Although some people thought I should try to keep the store going, I was very clear about what was mine to do—and this was *not* on my to-do list.

The historic building that David Smith & Co had occupied all these years was a Seattle destination. The spacious warehouse was a magical place, with its antique furniture, colorful pillows, exotic scents, and prayer flags. I could not bear to go to the auction; I didn't want to watch as the vultures swooped in to pick unceremoniously from the carcass David had left behind.

After the auction was over, however, I did Tend the Field of this beautiful space and our community through a final memorial event for David. Many people arrived from so many different phases of his life, most still stumbling through the whiplash confusion of how the upbeat and eccentric David they knew could have taken his own life. I had collected many of his books from around the house and put them on a large table with a sign inviting people to take a book with them as a connection to him. Anyone who knew David also knew that he was a lover of ideas, and there was something so intimate and touching about the way people ran their hands over the books that day, selecting which one would be their David keepsake.

As for the sale of the house—that would prove to be a very interesting journey. The monthly mortgage on the house was way more than I could afford on my own, and after several conversations with lawyers and accountants I decided that the best strategy was to not pay the mortgage for the next few months and move quickly to sell the house. That meant that I would need to price it carefully—not too low, but low enough to sell fast.

It took a great deal of discernment and jostling with the real estate agents before I finally felt I had the right agent and the right price. The letters and calls from the Bank of America got nastier and nastier as time went on. I stopped answering the house phone number and braced myself every time I walked out to the mailbox. The clock was ticking and I knew it . . . foreclosure was the hound nipping at my heels.

The first interest in buying the house came from a couple who were connected to a spiritual group of another friend. It seemed so synchronous that they would find their way to this sacred place and I waited for the offer to come in, sure that they would be the ones. It was the spring equinox, and it all seemed meant to be.

When their offer came in, however—at a fire sale price—I was dumbstruck and royally pissed off. I had already priced our extraordinary sanctuary way below its true value, and they had to know that. The price was so far below the asking amount that I could only imagine that they had heard of David's financial mess and thought they could grab it for a steal. It felt so disrespectful to me.

When my real estate agent relayed the offer, she said, "Well, it is certainly not what we would have expected. I will write them back tomorrow and let them know that we won't be accepting this offer."

Sometimes when Tending the Field we discover a strong *no* that needs to be declared for the sake of an equally strong *yes*. I could feel the anger rising through my body as I said, "Let's write them back right now to say that we will not be accepting this offer, nor any other offer they might make in the future. I want them to know that this offer is a total insult!"

With these words I was also speaking aloud to myself and the world, saying, "I may be broken and I may be vulnerable right now, but I am not a victim, and I still have the power of choice. I will sell this estate for the asking price, or I will lose everything trying."

By this point, my go-to phrase—from the movie *Mommie Dearest*, given to me by my good friend David early in the nightmare—was, "Don't fuck with me, fellas, this ain't my first time at the rodeo!"

I felt myself rising up in the face of the uncertainty, not grabbing the first little thing that came my way but rather trusting in the generous nature of life. I was standing in my own true authority—not making a choice out of fear but rather patiently waiting for a buyer who could take over the stewardship of this property and would pay the full asking price so that I could pay off some of David's debts to family and friends. And maybe then, if I was lucky, I would be able to receive funds from the state with which to start my new life.

I held firm to this clear intention—and every time fear and doubt entered, I reminded myself that I lived in a friendly universe and this would all work out. But living in a cardboard box under a bridge didn't feel that far away either.

And then a miracle occurred.

A year earlier, when David and I had tested out the idea of selling the property by putting it on the market for four months at a higher price than I was offering it at now, a woman had found the ad while browsing through estate sales in the Pacific Northwest. Our place had stood out to her as a magical and Zenlike sanctuary—but she was no heiress, and this search for an estate was just a kind of fantasy dream hobby she had. She and her husband were humble healers using various body practices to help people awaken consciousness and heal wounds from the past.

She'd returned to this site again and again, whenever she needed to be inspired by beauty. And then, suddenly, it was gone. Realizing it wouldn't sell during the winter, David and I had taken it off the market in November.

When it reappeared several months later at a substantially reduced price, she thought it was a sign.

A wealthy client and friend of hers happened to come in for a session that day, and the woman told her about the incredible property she had found a year ago and how she felt the price coming down so low was a direct sign to her. In a matter of days, the friend had decided to visit the property with the idea that she might buy it. The healers would live there full time, and the owner would come and visit when she could.

It was a new moon, with several propitious and encouraging planetary alignments, when they all came from Arizona to visit. I Tended the Field as best I could: I prepared everything for them, invited the beings of the property to welcome the potential new owners, and then left the property so that they could feel it as theirs.

The offer came in, strong and unequivocal, the same day. Strangely, the earlier house buyers, seeing what they had missed out on, also put another offer in that same day. Their offer was even stronger, with no requirement for fixing anything after inspection, but I was clear that I did not want to sell to them unless I had to and prayed that the people from Arizona would come in without any contingencies.

They did, thank goodness.

Synchronously, I signed the papers with the new owner in May, one hour after I returned from facilitating the opening retreat of the program that had originally been scheduled to launch just six days after David's death.

The trauma of my life had also greatly impacted the cohort of fourteen women who had committed to the life-changing work of our Mysterial program. At the beginning of every opening retreat, echoing the Persephone/Demeter myth, we ritually take women over a threshold to signify the choice to go into the underworld to do the deep work of transformation. When I was prematurely pulled into Hades before the program launched, everyone else was too—but the faculty team did an amazing job of creating a holding container as we all tumbled down. Tending the Field, they rearranged schedules, sent bimonthly emails with simple practices, and activated our online space early so everyone could connect. By the time we reached the opening retreat four months later, our hearts were already broken open to one another and our Circle field was deep and fertile.

Although in May I was still very much in the midst of the trauma of David's death, I knew it was vital that our work carry on and that I Tend the Field by being at the retreat. This was the commitment I had made when I was told David had taken his life, swearing to myself and the universe that I would not let his suicide destroy me or the work I was meant to do.

In our Mysterial programs we work with the limiting belief of the Hero archetype, *"I have to do to be of value,"* which can so often push us to act in ways that are not aligned or correct for us. It was a huge stretch for me to hold both my vulnerable, shattered self and my role as a Mysterial guide for the women who had chosen this journey, but I was living into the liberating belief of *"I am empowered to do what is mine to do,"* and I knew this was mine to do.

With a potent opening to the program complete and with the fires of my own work in the world lit again, I returned to Vashon after the retreat to release my home. It was a new moon again, a time that so many other important events would also synchronously occur on. The dark of the moon, an invitation to let go and plant seeds for the future. I sat in the living room with my friend Sharleen by my side and the new owner across from us and I signed the papers. A cycle had been completed.

The day that I left the property for good, the new managers of the estate met with me for a simple and beautiful ritual in the Kudus House. We began by smudging the space and ourselves with sage. After we'd dropped into a meditative state, I spoke the words that came to me: "I call in all the beings at all levels on this property—the plants, the stones, the birds, the animals, the buildings—I gather up all that David has stewarded all these years and that passed into my hands, and I offer it now to the new stewards. May you carry forward and magnify the energy of this beautiful sanctuary."

With those words, my job of Tending the Field of our sanctuary was complete. I rang my singing bowl and passed them the keys. It was done.

Now I would need to make my path by walking into the new world that awaited me.

Chapter 11:

Meta-Capacity—

Energy Stewardship

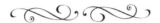

In the pressured times in which we live these days, we must all learn to manage our energy so that we have the capacity to *be with* all the stresses, joys, and challenges of life in a sustainable way. We need to learn how to wisely guide the movement and flow of our life force. The old, hypermasculine model that most of us have been schooled in has built into it the value of doing more and more to earn your place in the world. And this has resulted in unprecedented levels of burnout, anxiety, and depression.

Energy Stewardship is an essential capacity if we are to move steadily through the intensity of personal and collective trauma. We need to respect our sensate, feeling selves—knowing when we need to rest and restore and when to push forward with creative actions. In my women's leadership programs, I taught a new model for how to live, love, and lead that cycles through four steps: Stillness, Connection, Action, and Release.

Using Energy Stewardship, we do not initiate with Action, as we have been conditioned to do, but with Stillness and Connection. The female body is the ultimate model for this—the darkness of the womb provides an environment in which growth and change can take place as the miracle of life unfolds. This capacity to consciously hold a space in which something can move from conception through the maturing form to the release of birth is a powerful model of Energy Stewardship.

It was obvious to me, early on after David's death, that the road ahead was going to be long and very rough. I knew that I would need to pace myself—honoring my body's need for rest and renewal, discerning what was mine to do and what to pass on to others. And I wanted my actions to arise from the ground of my being as much as possible, so that I could be productive in a sustainable way. My personal container of morning practices—journaling, mediation, intention holding, ritual, exercise—was an essential structure for starting my days in connection to myself, helping me discern what actions were mine to take. (See appendix for a suggested series of Morning Flow Practices.) And I learned again and again at the end of the day's cycle of action how to release and drop back into Stillness.

An Evolutionary Invitation:
Energy Stewardship

Read the words below and let them evoke your body, heart, mind, and soul. Imagine yourself as a woman on the edge of evolution expressing Energy Stewardship.

To be still while still moving
Is how you walk through the world
Honoring the cycle of rest as much as you welcome
The excitement of doing

When you feel the call into action
Your dynamic nature rises up like a well-stoked fire
A flaming arrow of agency piercing the world

After the thrill of movement you rest back into
The quiet vessel of your being
Letting the well refill with the clear, sweet waters of essence

The creative cycle that guides you begins in stillness,
Moves to connection,
And then to action,
Before the release and return again into emptiness

Effortless effort is your signature
As what you do flows from you like a river
No overdoing or holding back

Your grounded center unwavering

A Proper Death

On the day David died, my cat, Emma, greeted me at the end of the path to our house with frantic meowing. This was the first visible sign that something was not right. David would never have left her out on her own if he was home. Her unsettled nature told me that this was no ordinary evening—in my gut, I knew then that things were not going to go well.

Emma and I found each other a couple of years after I moved to Seattle. Although I grew up with dogs and cats, I was too much of a wild spirit and traveler to commit to caring for a pet. But as Robert and I settled down in the USA, the idea of having animals began to seem less daunting. A good friend of mine lived with her two cats a few blocks away—an unpredictable orange tabby and a shy gray street cat—and I loved to play with them when visiting. We talked about what it took to care for cats and how it was relatively easy compared to dogs.

The idea of getting a cat was already percolating in my consciousness when one day a skinny cat appeared at my back door. She had a beautiful white nose, throat, and paws, striking gray tabby strips on her back, and sea green eyes that looked right into my soul. She seemed desperate to get into the house. Over the next few days, I fed her at the back door. Every morning, she would eat the food and look longingly into the house. She was shy and tentative, but seemed far too delicate and domesticated to be a feral cat.

I asked around the neighborhood about her and discovered that she had appeared recently and started to sleep on my next door neighbor's porch at night. I took a photo and put up posters to see if anyone recognized her.

After a week went by with no response, I decided to let her in.

The moment I opened the door, this dear, sweet, abandoned cat ran inside, upstairs, and under the bed. She seemed to know already where the safest place would be. It took time and patience for her to settle in with Robert and me.

Carl Jung was one of my inspirations, and I had been reading about his wife, Emma, when this little kitty arrived. Emma Jung was a remarkable woman who not only supported (both financially and emotionally) the deep inner excavations her husband was engaged in, but was also a noted analyst on her own.

I named my cat after her, and Emma became my deepest ally and support through all the years of her life. She was a very sensitive feline presence. She loved to sit with me when I meditated, read quietly, or played music. She had a particular thing for the sound of my soprano recorder; when I played it, she would rub her body against it and put her little nose right up at my mouth where the sounds were coming from. Whenever I wanted to call her or find her I would just play my recorder and she would come running from wherever she was.

Emma settled into a place in my heart that no creature had ever occupied before—and she taught me about how to steward my energy. If I was working at home, every afternoon around 3:00 p.m. she would come to find me for our nap together. She would cuddle into my belly, purring, as I rubbed behind her ears—and soon, we would both drift off into the Yin nectar land of a nap.

Before Emma came along, I was still struggling with a long-term tendency to overextend myself and hyperfunction to the point of burnout. These daily naps taught me how to replenish my energy so I could sustain longer and more productive stretches of creative output.

Emma and I had fourteen loving years together. Through all the changes in my life during those years, she was the steady presence.

David was decidedly not an animal person. He was a recluse in some ways, and the idea of caring for another being—human or animal—was foreign to him. But Emma worked her way into his heart, especially because of how she liked to sit above his right shoulder on a ledge in his office when he meditated. The two of them would get into wonderful bliss states together, and he came to love her.

So when I came down the path toward our house and saw Emma standing on the stone entry bridge with that same desperation to get inside that I had seen in her eyes and heard in the anxious pleading of her voice when I'd first met her, a chill of dread went through my body.

The rest of that night was a blur, as I have already described, but I imagine that Emma was upstairs in the quiet of the bedroom while everybody was coming and going in the chaos and shock of searching for and ultimately finding David.

When sometime after midnight, with my whole world shattered, I got into bed with two dear girlfriends on either side of me, Emma came up and wrapped herself around my head, the only spot left for her. As a shy cat, she did not know what to do with the other people in the bed, but she did know that I needed her, so she took up her position. She was still there in the morning when I woke into the nightmare of my new life.

—⁓—

For the next many months, there was so much change and disruption for Emma—the house being staged for selling, many new people in our home staying with us, and of course my own waves of grief, anger, fear. She missed David and in the first few weeks would often sit in his office on the ledge where she used to perch when he meditated. Sometimes I wondered if David's spirit was visiting and if the two of them were still grooving together in their bliss states.

With everything that was going on, it took me a few months to notice that Emma's appetite wasn't what it used to be, and that she was shrinking in size and beginning to have difficulty walking. She was already a delicate cat, but now she was frail.

The vet did tests and had no conclusive answers other than to say that this was likely cancer and unless I wanted to do aggressive treatments—which she didn't suggest, given Emma's age—I should just put her on steroids to minimize the discomfort for the remaining days of her life. She said that I would know when Emma was ready to go, and when that time came she could help release her from her body.

How would I ever know the right time to let go of my closest companion who had been with me through everything over the past fourteen years? And how could I even imagine doing that when I had just lost my beloved David and was about to lose my home? Could my heart possibly handle this loss without me dissolving into nothingness? Would I too want to glide over to the other side to be with both of them?

Even though we had such an energetic connection and she had been such a teacher for me in regulating and stewarding my own energy, I wasn't sure I could do the same for her. And I was quite sure that I would not know when was the right time for her to go.

Until I did. Until one morning a week before I was to leave my home, my community, and my life as I knew it.

I woke up that morning and Emma's frail body was barely moving on the special bed of blankets I had made for her. I thought she was already dead. But then her eyes blinked open and looked into mine and I heard her say, "It is time. I cannot go with you into this new life. My body is dissolving. You will be okay now. Please release me."

I sat with her, sobbing, and knew what I needed to do.

And so I called my cat whisperer friend Dianne to come be with me, and then I called the vet.

———

That last morning, while I waited for the vet to come, I carried Emma outside and laid her on the ground of the land she loved so much.

Bodhi, a feral cat that had woven his way into our lives a few years before, came over to be near her as soon as I laid her on the ground. Bodhi lived outside but would come over for meals and to visit Emma. Over the years she had learned to tolerate this scruffy wild black tomcat—but he loved her unabashedly, and always wanted to be nearby when she would let him.

I backed away from where I'd lain Emma down so that Bodhi could get as close as he wanted to her. He slowly approached, moving forward a few feet at a time and then sitting down as though checking to see if it was still alright with her that he was getting closer. She had barely enough energy to look up at him, but I believe she gave him the go-ahead to come and sit nearby.

In the end, he laid down about one foot away, and didn't try to play with her or get any closer. It was like he knew his place. Like he, too, was holding vigil.

The two of them were there in the sun for over an hour.

———

When the vet arrived, I carried Emma upstairs. The vet knew exactly how to be with me during these last moments and unobtrusively set everything slowly in motion. I sat on our bed with Emma on my lap and Dianne at my feet. I had already had my last conversation with Emma privately, thanking her for walking through this life with me.

As she lay quietly on my lap, I played my recorder for her one last time, hoping it would be the musical river she could ride to the other side. When the drugs kicked in, I saw the lifeforce gently leave her body. I bowed my head and silently wept. When I could move again, I slowly stood with her in my arms, placed her body in a bed of roses on the window seat where she often sat, and lit candles all around her.

I left her that way overnight to allow her spirit to transition sweetly to other dimensions. In the morning we did the final burial ritual—in the garden beside my sacred pear tree, symbol of the Divine Feminine. As we carried her body outside, Bodhi appeared at the top of the path, like a sentinel, and stood guard while we put her into the ground. Later, after we had left, he would come and sit beside her grave for long stretches of time. He missed her too.

———

I thought Emma's death would shatter me into too many pieces to ever go back together again. And yet something else quite surprising happened.

With David's death I had been slammed up against the impenetrable wall of loss through no choice of my own, stuck on this side with the living when the one I loved most was on the other side.

The same thing had occurred with my mother's sudden death eight days before my thirtieth birthday. I was at a spiritual community in British Columbia when I received an unexpected call from my father. He and I had not spoken for many months, and his voice cracked as he said, "Dear . . . your mother is dead."

How could I let in these impossible and final words, how could they be real? My mother was the one who had always seen past the great pretender that impressed so many others and called me back into the peace of my own authenticity. She was the outer representation of my inner center, the one I would come back to after all my wild adventures. She was the one who lived Energy Stewardship and knew how to pulse into action and when to rest back and recover.

When my mother was ripped from my world with no warning, the pain of it froze the tender parts of myself and tempered me for the world of business. Her death set me adrift from the Feminine ground of my being for many years to come and swung me into the world of doing, striving, achieving.

Both David's and my mother's death had been my only experiences of death until now, and they both had been characterized by shock and trauma. Emma's death was the first time that I had ever walked with another up to the threshold between this world and the next, stewarding my energy wisely while also being able to help steward hers into a peaceful transition. It was hard, and yet it was holy ground. It was her final gift to me.

Two days later I drove away from my island sanctuary, my life as I knew it, and my darling Emma, lying peacefully beneath the pear tree.

Chapter 12:

Meta-Capacity—

Authentic Presence

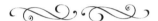

The longing to express ourselves fully and honestly without the false self-censoring of our expression naturally rises to the surface during trauma and loss. There is simply not enough energy available to pretend to be anyone or anything other than who you are in the moment. The shattering of the ego during the dark times can be an opening to something much larger if we let it occur and allow our true nature to shine through in an Authentic Presence.

This kind of vulnerable transparency is a powerful currency in a world that is shifting and changing so fast. If we can't be true to ourselves and find that inner anchor, then we have little chance of being an inspiring agent of change for others. When you meet a person who is truly themselves, you can't help but be drawn in by their overwhelming genuineness. It is our authentic presence that actually creates room for others to be themselves. When we set ourselves free, we set others free as well.

From the first morning I awoke after David's suicide, I was committed to being real with myself and with others. I simply had no desire to put up masks, play games, or pretend to be some heroic version of myself. I discovered how much energy I had been putting into creating a persona that was competent, smart, independent, and had it all together. In the absence of that ego efforting, I was left with a deeper sense of permission to be exactly who I was at any moment.

An Evolutionary Invitation:
Authentic Presence

Read the words below and let them evoke your body, heart, mind, and soul. Imagine yourself as a woman on the edge of evolution expressing Authentic Presence.

Finally you stand firmly on the ground of your being
In the quiet immensity of your own presence

Deeply at ease with who you are
You have come to love your broken open, imperfectly perfect self

On the shore of this new land,
You look out at a very different world
Safe and at ease, there is no need to hide

Your essence, rising up like sap from your roots,
Moves through you and out into the world in one fluid stream

The false masks fall away and your true face
Meets the world's gaze with love
Awake and full with all your senses,
Yet spacious enough for others
You are so much yourself, you see by the
Radiant light of your own darkness

Who Am I Now?

Once I had sold our sanctuary on Vashon and the reality of that loss settled into my bones, I knew that the most important thing for me going forward would be to find a true sanctuary, a place where I could feel safe and at home. I also knew that I would need to leave the island for Seattle. I wanted to be free of the projections of my wonderful community on Vashon—the long, sad, sideways glances at me when I would enter Thriftway, the looks that said, even if their words did not, *How could David have done this to you, and what will become of you now?*

It was going to be hard enough to move forward into the unknown without having the cloak of shame or despair being constantly reinforced by people who knew the story. I did not want to be just "the dead guy's wife." I wanted room to discover who I was becoming in this emergent phase of my life.

Home has always been important to me. Cozy, beautiful, and inviting places are central to my signature presence. I would need to call this next nest into being so that it could hold and nurture my most authentic nature in this liminal time of dismantling and recreating myself. To do this, I used a process that I had taught to women in my programs—a process for activating the "field of all potentialities."

In this predominantly hypermasculine world, many of us do not know how to access the potent capacity of the imaginal realms. When you hold something vividly as an image and you activate the feelings in your body connected with the picture of the future you want, you activate the energetic fields that surround you. This sets up an imaginal wave that changes the electron balances of the ecosystem around you so that what you really wish for begins to manifest. In other words, a deeply held image is literally a "seed planted in the fields that surround us," as scholar, philosopher, and visionary Jean Houston metaphorically describes it.

So I created an image board. I bought numerous home magazines, some of which surprised me and yet felt authentic to who I was becoming now, and I spent a few days cutting out the pictures that really inspired and energized me. And then, one night, I lit a candle, played soothing music, and began to move the images around on a poster board until I got into a flow state and saw a pattern emerging that felt like me—or at least the me I might become.

I left my image board out on the table over the next couple of weeks, and every now and again I would play with it—adding images, removing ones that no longer resonated, and shifting them around on the board. I was waiting for the pattern to feel fully, authentically me. When it got there, I glued everything down.

I had a small rectangular teak table in my office that I had designated as my altar of the future. It was a home base—a true north—for me as I navigated through all the challenges and chaos surrounding me. Daily, I would light a candle, hold my intentions for the future, and take in the images I had on the small table—a photo of David, as I was not ready to let him go yet; Kuan Yin, the goddess of Compassion; small antique Buddha statues that David had collected in Asia; photos of my family and friends; a heart stone David had given me; crystals and rare stones that I had gathered throughout my life from different places in the world; and a small vase of fresh flowers that I replaced weekly, a reminder to tend this garden of my future. And now I added in my beautiful future *Home for Authentic Presence* vision board.

Every morning and every time I walked by my altar, I let myself totally see, touch, taste, and feel myself in this new home. I took a photo of the vision board and sent it to my friends, asking them to forward it on to others who might know of a place in Seattle that matched this description. I sent the image out into the field of all possibilities, and then I made trips into Seattle to start looking at places.

There was nothing. Nothing. It was depressing and discouraging. Seattle was in a boom period, and the rentals were limited and horrible. But I held my vision nonetheless.

Then, one day it happened. Trish, someone whom I had recently met, and who had known David, was about to sell her home in the very neighborhood I was interested in. She was going to sell it to the couple who lived next door as an investment property for them.

When I spoke with her on the phone and she asked if I wanted to come and see it I got a rush of full-body tingles—a sign that this might be the place.

I walked down the pathway, between ginkgo trees and lush green ferns, to her house and knew instantly that this was my next home. It was a modern, two-story house with an atrium in the center through which the sun streamed in. In many ways it was a "mini-me" version of my larger home on Vashon, with lots of light and tall glass doors. It was also a kind of sanctuary, but in contrast to my Vashon property, with its wide, expansive views, this was secluded and tucked away. This was so perfectly aligned with my authentic experience of this being a time to pull inside and heal. And in the secret garden backyard was a separate studio with tall glass folding doors that opened out onto a peaceful garden. It would become my office—the place I could write this book, and begin to work with clients again when the time was right.

The home was perfect, its similarity to my image board uncanny. I knew it was meant to be mine—a gift from the friendly universe to let me know that I would have a sanctuary base from which to rebuild my life from scratch. But it was expensive. How could I do it?

A miracle occurred. Trish negotiated with the women who were buying the house from her, and they generously agreed to start me out with a lower rent than they knew they would get if they put it on the market. And then Trish offered to pay the difference for a year between what I could afford now and the rent the owners would need.

The generosity and kindness of these three women touched me to the core. Their confidence that I would get on my feet again and be in a very different position in a year was itself a gift. It meant everything to me. I thought I would be in the house for just a couple of years, but nine years later I am still here, completing this book.

The surround of this beautiful home, my kind neighbor land-ladies, and my best friends living nearby was an essential container into which I would slowly unfurl my Authentic Presence in the months and years ahead. It was exactly what I needed to find my way back to myself and to move back into the world.

A few months after David died, someone contacted me about being one of the keynote speakers at an Emerging Women event in Seattle. It was scheduled for August, and I remember naively thinking, when I was asked, that by then I would be back to work and doing what I loved to do.

Speaking is one of the things that strikes terror into many. But for me it is the opposite. I love nothing more than tuning in to a room full of people and sharing what I know, awakening new possibilities. Emerging Women was an initiative supporting women to become a force for change in the world. Everything about the organization and the event seemed aligned with who I was and the work that I was doing.

The closer I got to the day of the event, the more I realized that the talk I had been planning on giving was simply not something I could deliver. The only way I could show up at this event authentically was if I spoke from the raw and vulnerable place that I was still very much in. I was terrified to do that—yet I knew that my Authentic Presence was all that I truly had to offer. In our Mysterial work we had uncovered a primary limiting belief of the Mother archetype, *"I am not enough,"* that was far too often a guiding unconscious narrative taking women away from the ground of authentic being. I could feel myself unwilling to be driven by this story and instead tuned my awarness to the liberating belief, *"I am enough just as I am."*

Onstage the day of the event, the host introduced me with a glowing resume of my women's leadership accomplishments. This was the ground that had brought me to this moment—but the place that I would speak from on this day was unexplored territory.

Before I stood up to walk onto the stage, I took a deep breath and tucked my notes under the seat. I was going to do this freefall, without a backup parachute, or not at all.

"The talk I am giving tonight is a very different talk than the one I thought I would make when I was asked to do this in early spring," I began, finding my presence in the bright stage lights before continuing on. "When I spoke with our host Chantal a few weeks ago and asked her what she might want me to share during this time she said—share your own leadership edge, what matters to you these days, not so much about your theories and models but your current experience of what it is that you teach. "

I stepped over to the righthand side of the stage and up to the very edge. I peered into the audience of over 400 women and continued.

"I was asked to speak to my own personal leadership edge, and this takes me to a very different place. Over here, my leadership edge has been more like a leadership cliff, off of which I was thrown when tragedy occurred in my life at the beginning of this year. Through these past eight months, I have taken all that I learned over there"—I pointed to the left side of the stage—"to another level of understanding and deepening, and I am now in very new territory over here."

Over the next few minutes, I invited the women in the room to come with me to this vulnerable edge, to trust that cultivating the deep Feminine ground of being *is* what allows us to go through the challenges of our lives. The seed potential for a Mysterial way of leading, I told them, needed to crack open so that we could break through to the next level of our capacity as women with Authentic Presence.

I explained that my own leadership edge had been to embrace this brutal cracking-open and to be vulnerable enough to share that experience on this very public stage. My brokenness had revealed my hidden wholeness. The shattering of the structures of my life had brought me closer to myself, to others, and to the world—had brought me to a place of greater compassion and love.

The room was by now deeply still, everyone with me in the poignancy of loss and the possibility of resilience cultivated through struggle, failure, and trauma.

I ended my talk by referencing the Leonard Cohen song "Anthem," which describes how the cracks in a thing are what let the light shine through. My invitation to women from the fragile edge of my own experience was to ask themselves, *What is cracking me open now? And what Authentic Presence might that be making more space for?*

I walked off the stage and back to my seat without the usual experience of being pumped up after delivering a speech. I was quiet inside, and still present to the tenderness of the experience of being so raw and so received at the same time.

Afterward, I had many women speak to me about how deeply they had connected with my story as a permission for their own failures, disappointments, and losses—with the idea that these experiences could in fact be the very pathway to a whole new level of Authentic Presence.

I knew after this talk that the path I was now walking, step by uncertain step, had the possibility of being a blessing for others. I laced up my hiking boots for the days ahead, as I knew the way I was taking—the way of the Mysterial woman—would not be a quick ascent but rather a steady pilgrimage through the darkness.

Part Three:

Return

Chapter 13:

Through Trauma to Transformation

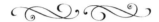

"Sometimes you have to take your own hand
as though you were a lost child
and bring yourself stumbling
home over twisted ice."

—Louise Erdrich

In part two I introduced you to each of the eight Meta-Capacities of a Mysterial Woman independently, and explained how I used and further refined those capacities through the fire of my traumatic situation. But the reality is that those capacities did not emerge in isolation; rather, they arose together in a synergistic and powerful Mysterial way of being.

The first nine months after David's death had their own unique challenges. There were so many things to do before I could really step into the next phase of my new life. By September, however, I could feel myself starting to walk onto new ground. The next eight years were a very different experience of recreating my life, in a new way and with eyes wide open.

In the chapters to follow, instead of highlighting the individual Mysterial Meta-Capacities, I will take you through a more synthesized way of walking the Mysterial path with all the capacities online at once—each one rising as needed in a natural integration.

————

With every day and every month, I grew more and more certain that I was forging a solid path over the charnel grounds of loss. I truly became a woman on the edge of evolution, living out beyond the distinctions that I had spent years determining. My inner Mysterial map was embodied, and I found my capacity to tune it as I went along—knowing when one archetypal energy or particular Meta-Capacity was needed. I made my path by walking, slowly and steadily, into the void, and as I did I discovered that the next stone I needed to step on always arose just as I swung my leg forward with faith.

Nine months after David's death, I knew that I needed to get away from everything and reset my system after all the enormous changes I had been through in such a short period of time. My brother, Peter, and his wife, Karen, were heading off on a guided bike trip of Puglia, Italy, and that sounded like the perfect escape and opportunity for a reset.

With the change in my business, I was also up against the clock: my new, somewhat barebones health plan would be kicking in right after I left for a month abroad, and the plan I was leaving had such great benefits that I was taking advantage of doing every kind of assessment I could before I transitioned. I checked my heart, tested my bones for osteoporosis, and did all the blood tests for a thorough annual exam. Last on the list was the simple mammogram.

I was very carefree about this test compared to the others. I had never had anything come up on a mammogram, and I had no family history of breast cancer. I wasn't a big fan of mammograms based on things I had read about false alarms and the effects of radiation, so it had been four years since my last scan.

I breezed into the Swedish Hospital Breast Imaging Center, ready to do the test, tick that procedure off my list, and be done.

I was taken through the usual breast flattening, stacking, and positioning for the various x-rays. No problem. When it was done, I waited in my special gown in the post-mammogram room for my results.

When the attendant came to get me, I assumed she was going to say, "Everything is fine, you can get dressed now."

Instead, she walked me into another office and said that they had found something and they just wanted to take another look at it with ultrasound, if that would be alright?

Seriously? I thought. *No, that would not be alright! I do not have breast cancer—and only a very, very sick universe would deal me the breast cancer card after everything else I've been through!*

After waiting an impossibly long time, I was finally taken into a freezing cold, dark ultrasound room, where a doctor investigated my left breast further with her special wand—but wasn't able to see anything more conclusive. "I don't see anything but a few calcifications with the ultrasound," she told me. "I am sorry but they are going to want you to do a needle biopsy just to be sure that there are no potentially cancerous cells lurking. It is very rare that these calcifications are anything, but this is our protocol. I'm so sorry to make you go through this."

A needle biopsy? Are you fucking kidding me?

—

Normally I would have taken the time to assess all of this a little more fully, but I had exactly seven days before I left for my bike trip, and my current health plan was set to end on the day of my departure.

So I managed to schedule myself in for this "simple" needle biopsy procedure three days later—except it was not so simple, it was a terrifying and painful process for an already traumatized woman: strapped to a machine, told not to move or breathe at all no matter what while a needle was thrust through my breast to both take some sample tissue and leave behind a staple so that we would remember the site of the strike and calcifications.

My breast was bruised and sore afterward, as they'd warned me it would be. I was relieved to have done the deed, however, and certain that now they would have what they needed and the case of potential breast cancer would be closed.

They told me it would take a few days to let me know the results, so I carried on preparing for my trip, mostly forgetting about it, as I was so sure that it was nothing.

The day before I was supposed to leave, I got a call from a doctor at Swedish Hospital. I was sitting in my car, parked near the grocery store, when the doctor said in a deadpan voice, "Well, we have looked at the results and we still can't tell what is happening. It looks like you have alien ductal . . . blah blah blah . . ."

I was already going into shock.

". . . Now, this isn't cancer, but these calcifications sometimes indicate that they could *become* cancerous. So it isn't really anything to worry about, but we would like you to do a surgical biopsy next week." She used the analogy of it being like a buoy on the water, marking where there are rocks. "We just want to go down and take a closer look at those rocks," she said in her indifferent and trans-actional voice.

Well, for sure this wasn't going to happen before I left for Italy the next day at 8:00 a.m.

When I got off the phone with the unsympathetic doctor, I immediately called one of my On Call Support girlfriends, Deborah. I was heading toward a panic attack—all I'd heard was "cancer" and "surgery," and with that I was over the threshold of what I could hold.

Deborah managed to talk me back down off the cliff and I was able to drive my car home.

———

One of my dearest friends, Virginia, who was coming over to help me pack for the trip, arrived shortly after I got home. Strangely, she had had the exact same thing occur to her the year before. When she reminded me of this, I vaguely remembered sending her energy when she went for her follow-up biopsy. She said that after all her work with various alternative healers between the first mammo-gram and the biopsy, they found absolutely nothing in the second mammogram. This was very reassuring, and I began to recenter myself around health and well-being and detach from the narrative of the C word.

I had just been through the massive trauma of my husband's suicide and losing everything I held most precious in my life. Of course my body would have some alien cells floating around, I realized. I decided that instead of jumping into a surgical biopsy I would augment my immune system, doing energy work and applying other alternative approaches to health, to be sure my body had the best possible chance to heal. I would go to Italy to rest and rehabilitate myself, not dive into surgery.

After I returned from Italy, I used all my ways of knowing to determine a path forward. I decided to bring together the best that medical science had to offer, input from trusted allies, and my own intuitive body wisdom. I consulted with the head of the Swedish Hospital Women's Cancer Center, Pat Dawson, an extraordinary physician who had been a student in one of my women's leadership programs. I consulted with my family full of physicians. I consulted a naturopath. I consulted an energy intuitive. And I met with an integrative medicine doctor who gave me a powerful way of looking at the mainstream medical diagnosis of alien ductal calcifications.

"It's like there is the idea that everyone who wears a black turtleneck is dangerous," she told me. "And so in case one of them turns out to be a killer, we want to kill them all first."

Ultimately, using all my ways of knowing, I chose not to do the surgical biopsy. And as it turned out, it would take me three years to be ready to do another mammogram. I prepared for the experience for weeks by holding the clear intention of a positive outcome and inviting others to hold that image with me. I also knew that given the trauma from my last visit, I needed to take my best friend Dianne with me so that I would feel supported as I walked again through the trauma field.

I received the results two days later. All clear!

——

When I made the many decisions that I had to make along the way around how I would engage with the medical system through my breast cancer scare, there was no certainty that the outcome would be so positive. It isn't that I am recommending that anyone else should follow this path. What I am saying is that instead of just blindly giving up our authority to the "outer experts" in moments of crisis, we need to stay grounded and present to ourselves so that we make the best possible decisions. When the stakes are high sometimes we just default to giving others our power. I elected instead, in this case, to choose the Mysterial Way and open myself to all the expertise and information available at all levels—and then, from a place of grounded knowing, make my path by walking.

Chapter 14:

Eat, Bike, Heal

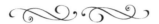

"No, no, there is no going back.
Less and less you are
that possibility you were.
More and more you have become
those lives and deaths
that have belonged to you."

—WENDELL BERRY

I sat back in my seat on the plane to Italy in an adrenal exhaustion, not just from the past nine months, but from the breast cancer scare of the last twenty-four hours. Tears streamed down my cheeks and my eyes stared blankly out the window as we pulled away from the earth below. I was so deeply sad, deeply lonely, and deeply relieved to be leaving everything behind, including the person who might have breast cancer.

I was going to reconnect with the me who had lived in Italy thirty-five years earlier. The me who had been a student of restoration architecture, in love with the world, full of hope and possibility for the future. I was also going to reconnect with the me who had been in Italy with David ten years earlier, celebrating my fiftieth birthday.

It had been our first trip together, and a fabulous exploration of art, beauty, and our awakening love.

Italy held so many positive memories for me. As I settled into my seat on the plane, I turned on an Italian language program I had downloaded on my phone and let the mellifluous words wash through me. Riffing off Liz Gilbert's *Eat Pray Love*, I dedicated this trip to Eat, Bike, Heal.

———

Peter, Karen, and I had flown in a few days before the bike trip to get over jet lag and spend some time visiting Puglia. We stayed in the historic eleventh century town of Conversano in a beautiful stone hotel with a Thermarium Spa. I was grateful to have these few days with family before meeting new people, and to begin to release myself from the contraction and action the last nine months had required of me.

I booked myself a massage treatment at the spa to drop into my body and arrive in this new reality of my life. In the locker room, I was given little disposable paper panties, a robe, and told to go up to the massage room.

A handsome young man was waiting for me in the massage room. He invited me to get on the table but did not leave the room. There were no discreet sheets that I could pull over me. He didn't avert his eyes. It was all very matter-of-fact. Now I remembered the me who used to live in Italy, who was comfortable in my body and who swam topless in the sea like everyone else.

He lathered me up with lavender-scented oil and began a sensual massage that caught me completely off guard. I was simply unprepared for this level of intimacy with a total stranger after all that I had been through. His hands roamed here and there, down my back in slow motion, along my sides, inside my thighs, spreading and lifting and bending my legs in positions that I had never tried before, even with adventurous lovers! I found myself thinking how glad I was that a few months before I'd had an unsightly sebaceous cyst removed from my back.

When he asked me to roll over and my bruised breast from the needle biopsy had full frontal exposure, I told him in no uncertain terms that my breasts were out of bounds. I am quite sure that they would have been well massaged had I not done that. Everywhere else was soon coated in oil as he slithered all over, one hand sometimes going up the inside of my thigh while the other moved slowly down the side of my breast and an elbow somewhere in between.

The culminating moment seemed to be when he had his hand on my belly and then put my hand on top of his and asked me where I wanted him to go next. As I was still fumbling around with my Italian, I wasn't quite sure what he meant, so I just let my hand go along with his wherever it was going—which ended up being around in circles on my belly like a car stuck in a roundabout, the driver not quite sure which exit to take.

He tried again to let me know that I could direct his hand to go anywhere and I suddenly realized where that somewhere was— down south! Instead, I turned the car north and told him my shoulders were so VERY, VERY sore.

It was clear that I had a long way to go before I would be able to welcome pleasure back into my body.

———

A few days later Peter, Karen, and I joined up with the rest of the bike group on our organized tour and headed off for the east coast of Puglia. It was exactly what I needed. Days spent on the road biking hard through exquisite landscapes; nights spent eating good food, drinking good wine, and laughing before dropping into bed exhausted.

Hardly anyone there knew the story of my recent trauma, and I did not share it. For these ten days I was a biker, a sister, a women's leadership consultant, and a lover of Italy.

At the close of a long day of biking near the end of the trip we arrived in the beautiful seaside town of Monopoli. We were all exhausted after one of the toughest rides of the trip along the beautiful, rugged coastline. When I went to bed that night, I fell into a deep liminal sleep as I breathed in the salty, cool breezes of the Adriatic Sea.

Finally, after months of trying to connect with him, David came to me in a dream.

It was the opening day of my new store and everyone was bustling around preparing things. There were colorful fabrics, pillows, and books in the front part of the store; farther back, beautiful objects from different places in the world were arranged to create a gorgeous aesthetic. I was energized and excited for this new beginning and was moving around the space, checking in here and there with people, fluffing the purple pillows, tending to the final touches.

At one point I went down a step and into the back of the store to get something. One of the women who worked for me came back and said there was someone who wanted to see me, if that was alright.

I looked up and standing just behind her was a man wearing one of David's signature indigo blue shirts from Bali. Then I realized it was David. My heart caught as I recognized him and a deep wave of grief and anxiety welled up in my chest. He looked at me with the steady gaze that I knew so well, but underneath I saw his shame and his timid approach, his fear of what I might say or do.

I was frozen in place. He walked slowly toward me and took me in his arms.

I did not resist. My whole being released into his embrace— I could suddenly feel all the stress, terror, and grief that I had been holding by myself dissipating into his loving arms. In the dream he had not died, but he had left me, and I'd thought I would never see him again.

And now here he was, so very sorry for leaving me and realizing that he never should have gone away and left me with everything. His love and remorse mixed together were a healing balm to my exhausted being.

After a few minutes in this loving embrace, I was

reminded of my store's opening. I told him that I had changed while he was away—that I had created this store, and it would be mine and successful.

And then I woke up from the dream crying.

It was very early morning and still dark outside—the gauzy white curtains were gently swaying in the breeze of the open window. I could hear the nostalgic caws of the seagulls and smell the sea air. Once I realized where I was and that David was not there with me, I tried desperately to reenter the dream. I wanted to be back in his arms, talking about everything that had happened and everything that lay ahead in front of us to do together.

But the door was shut and I could not go back in.

This was the first time since he had left that I'd felt he was truly there with me—not through someone else but directly. When our eyes had met, I'd seen that gaze of his that always brought me home to myself. In his strong arms I felt so safe and loved. I could feel his remorse and his grief at all the pain he had caused me. And I knew that I was still his beloved.

My heart broke further open, my body heaved with sobs, and I curled into the fetal position. I tried to anchor in my body the feelings of relief, of gratitude for his remorse, of not being alone, and of the sweetness of our love as the sun slowly rose outside my window. What had been given to me in the dream when I entered his world would have to be enough in mine.

I would drink often from this memory reservoir in the difficult days ahead. I understood the dream not just as a connection with David but also as a message for me about finding the thread of my own destiny and rebuilding my life.

———

After the bike trip, Peter and Karen returned home to Canada and I traveled on by train to Assisi. When I had lived in Florence many years earlier, Assisi had been one of my favorite places to visit, both for its beautiful architecture and for the sacred presence of St.

Francis of Assisi I felt there. I had decided to stay at a Yogananda retreat center in the mountains above the town itself. Although I did not have a direct connection to this spiritual path, the book *Autobiography of a Yogi* by Yogananda had been one of the most impactful catalysts for my own spiritual growth many decades earlier. A friend had introduced me to Dana, an American woman who lived at the retreat center and was doing process art as a healing therapy. I thought the combination of being in a spiritual community and working with the visual and imaginal realms would be healing.

I stayed in a small cottage near the main community building and settled into my own rhythm—working with Dana, going to meditation sessions, and eating my meals in the communal dining room.

The first day I worked with Dana, she led me through a guided meditation into the realms of imagination and then she invited me to paint the shapes and colors I had seen onto a large piece of art paper. Using big, fat brushes, she guided me to let my body and heart express onto the blank page.

I spontaneously drew a tree-like form with deep roots and branches reaching up into the heavens with a bold red spiral moving from the center of the tree and spiraling up and out around the page. Later, when Dana guided me to explore the image through movement and asked it to speak to me, the words it spoke were "You are free." There was something I was beginning to see about the freedom possible when I connected with my own desire and needs as well as those of others. I had lived so much of my life with a sense of responsibility for others and for the world without much care for myself.

This had certainly played out with David. It was as though through the shattering experience of loss I had come home to myself in a deeper way and I was just beginning to discover the freedom in this new consciousness.

One of my oldest and dearest friends from my early life living in a spiritual community, Merle, came to join me for a few days, as she had just finished teaching a writing workshop in Venice. I rented a sporty little red Fiat 500 that reminded me of the first car I owned in Florence, which was then called a Cinquecento, and went to the train station to pick her up. Freedom!

It was comforting to be with Merle's grounded, Mother Earth essence. She was one of the few friends still in my life who knew me before David and had also met him and been present at our wedding. We had a couple of days to zip around in my car, visit the historic sites, listen to some sacred music, and take advantage of the sulfur healing baths nearby. After nine months in a cocoon of trauma, it felt liberating to experience all these new things with a dear friend.

I knew that David's birthday on October 20 would be hard for me, so I had arranged for us both to experience a powerful sound healing session that day with Michel, a gifted healer who was part of the Yogananda community. It was the perfect way to move through that difficult day—a day that reminds me of the blessing of David's birth and the pain of his leaving.

I have always had a deep connection to music and sound healing, and I instinctively knew that it could be very helpful in the healing of my trauma. My experiences with sound healing in the past had taught me how the vibrations of different instruments could move stuck energy. The bike trip had already shaken some things loose at the gross physical level, and I trusted that the session with Michel could powerfully shift things at the subtle level.

Michel's studio was filled with a multitude of exotic instruments—crystal bowls, enormous gongs, Tibetan singing bowls, gamelans, stringed instruments. He invited me to share with him what had brought me in for a session. He was French and I immediately felt comfortable sharing, in a mix of French and English, about the trauma I had been through and was seeking to release through this session. I also told him that I wanted to honor David, on his birthday, by releasing myself from carrying the trauma of his death.

Michel invited me to stand behind his enormous eight-foot Chinese gong and he began to slowly play it, increasing the speed bit by bit. The combination of striking force, striking sequence, and striking rhythm, coupled with the oscillatory wave motion of the resonating gong, all contributed to a stunning experience. I could literally feel the cells of my body vibrating.

Then he handed me the padded mallet and told me to let myself be guided by my inner impulse to find the rhythm and volume of sound that my body needed. After one or two swings of the mallet, it seemed like I went into a trance and the gong and I were one. The gong played me, and it played me hard and loud. Like my journey into the volcanic crater of Haleakalā in Maui, there was something deeply healing about being met by a sound and vibration that matched my inner state. I screamed and sobbed, letting the sound purge me of all I was still holding. At a certain point the energy shifted suddenly and I transformed into a Samurai warrior, turning the pain into a forging fire. A strength and fierceness rose up in me—a Kali energy burning away some of the karma of this whole experience. I finished with a final, slow tapping at the center of the gong and eventually settled into silence.

Michel guided me to lie down on his warm sound table, underneath which were many stringed instruments, crystals, and Tibetan bowls. He played them in an ongoing wave of sound that came up from the ground and seemed to wash all around me. My whole body tingled as my energy smoothed out and eventually went quiet. When Michel was done I stood up, rang a beautiful Tibetan bowl, and offered a blessing to David on this day of his birth.

⌣

After the sound healing ceremony, I felt ready to go back to Seattle and into my new life there.

A few weeks after I returned home from Italy, I finally had a session with Lynn Austin, a gifted channeler, and for the first time I actually felt that David was there with me. Perhaps it had taken our connection in the dreamworld for me to be open to him in this way.

Speaking through Lynn, David named people and places that she could not possibly have known. He mentioned his beloved sister,

Pam, and his brother-in-law, Don, and talked about how sorry he was to have hurt them both. He spoke through Lynn to say that his mother, Mary Ellen, who had died the year before him, had met him when he crossed over, and he also wanted to convey his love for his niece Claire and nephew Peter.

The level of detail was remarkable. Through Lynn, David told me that there was an energetic opening on January 3 to leave and that he could not resist it. He was simply done and had no strength left to continue on. He also said that he stayed as long as he could—an extra ten years longer than his incarnation agreement—because of his love for me. And he told me I would get through this and that joy and a new love would be possible for me.

The connection felt reassuring and confusing at the same time. I did not want a new love, and I could not imagine being happy again.

I met with Lynn every few months for the next couple of years, and each time David would reassure me that everything was working out. The impulse to try to find and connect with the person who is suddenly gone from your life is so instinctual. For me, the act of trying was a way to gradually be able to accept the reality that I would never be with him again in this dimension. That in itself was healing.

I wanted to believe that David was still tracking my life here on earth—that now and again he was sending little blessings my way and making my path a little easier. During the first few years after his death, each time something miraculous occurred, I wondered if he was helping. At the same time, I did not want to give him too much credit when I was the one doing all the hard work.

One thing I knew for sure was that the veil between the realms was ripped open in his leaving, and what I felt and saw through the thin gossamer had changed me. It had brought me more firmly onto this earth and my choice to be here—in good times and in bad.

Chapter 15:

Deep Dive into the Shadows

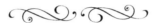

> *"The psychological rule says that*
> *when an inner situation is not made*
> *conscious, it happens outside as fate."*

> —CARL JUNG

I've come to understand some things over these past nine years about trauma and loss—and to realize that many of us have to approach the healing needed after life-shattering experiences in stages.

At first there is the tumble down into the underworld and the invitation to not resist and to be present with what is. This takes time. Slowly your eyes begin to adjust and you learn to see in the dark. Eventually, you will have enough capacity to turn toward the hidden corners and face the shadows waiting there.

It was Carl Jung who first used the term "shadow" to describe those parts of the self that are hidden from conscious view and are not experienced as an aspect of who we are. In our early, formative years we learn that in order to get love, safety, and belonging we must disown parts of ourselves that don't result in those attachment needs being met. So we do what any wise child would do—we hide those aspects of ourselves away by removing them from our conscious awareness, tucking them into the shadows. These "unacceptable" parts of ourselves stop developing and stay frozen in time, never getting a chance to grow up. What should have been our shining (self-esteem, joy, wisdom, etc.) becomes our shadows. And our gnarly bits, too (fear, anger, shame, etc.), get disowned and stowed away down in the dark, only to erupt in unpredictable, self-sabotaging ways.

As I approached the one-year anniversary of David's death, I knew I was ready for the next stage of my healing—that it was time to do my own deeper shadow work. I wanted to make sure that whatever I needed to learn and see from this experience got integrated into my consciousness, so that I would not have to receive another harsh wake-up call. I would need to find someone to hold me in the way that I could hold others—someone with a deep archetypal understanding of trauma and shadows.

I found a powerful ally in Norma, a depth psychologist trained in the shamanic arts.

In our first session together I told her that I was ready to do the shadow work required so that I could find the hidden parts of myself—the dark and the light—that might be available now after my dismembering and the dismantling of my life. I wanted to fully face the brutal offering of this experience and, as I approached David's death day of January 3, to be sure that I held myself in the alchemical fire of transformation so that I could understand what this tragedy was about for me.

I knew that this shadow work piece was vital to find my confidence and sovereignty as Queen Persephone, who had gone through the darkest night of the soul and then arisen with more authenticity, wisdom, and compassion because of it. I wanted to be able to transition into the next phase of my life experiencing the wound of this time as a tender place of opening and not an albatross around my neck. I wanted to gather up all the pieces of this journey—conscious and unconscious—so that I could be fully present for whatever would be next. I wanted to allow the phoenix of my new self to arise authentically from the ashes of my old one.

To get there, I would need to use the light of my conscious mind to travel deeper into the unconscious shadowlands.

I began the journey by articulating my intention. I knew that if I was to go down into the dark consciously, I would need to have clarity about what was at stake, like a belay line hooking me to the Upper World. My intention was the reason I was willing to turn toward the dark and descend to deeper realms. I wrote it down:

I intend to embody my sovereign seat in the world in loving partnership with others enabling me to source a life that is deeply fulfilling and abundantly generative.

In one of the first shamanic journeys that Norma guided me into, I found an animal ally who still journeys with me today: the Black Panther. After the imaginal experience with Norma, I did some research into this power animal and discovered why she was sent to me. A symbol of the dark Mother, the dark face of the moon, the Panther is all about reclaiming one's true power and rebirth from the darkness. I would need this energy to turn toward the shadow patterns.

I spent some time in my visual journal collaging images of the Black Panther I had found online, and I bought a beautiful statue to put on my altar while I did this work.

After months of deep inquiry through dialogue with Norma, tracking my dreams, and journaling, I came to recognize a pattern that had been present in my life long before David but had definitely played out with him: feeling abandoned.

I'd had such a deep sense of belonging with David, and then he'd abandoned me. My mother, the other person with whom I had such a deep sense of belonging, had also left me suddenly. But my deep sense of not belonging in this world went back to the very beginning of my life. My mother's sister, Aunt Betsy, had told me long after my mother died that when I was born as the second girl after my older sister, my father had been so angry with my mother that I was not a boy that he'd refused to speak with her for ten days. I found it hard to believe that anyone would do that, but my aunt said that my mother had told her about this experience and how devastating it was to feel his rejection of both me and her.

I didn't know for sure what actually happened, but I did know that I have always lived with a core wound of a sense of not belonging. It was not lost on me that my life's work was about helping women to welcome all of themelves and claim their rightful and equal place on the earth. It is often the case that our wounded places become the opportunities for our healing and then, if we are willing to transform the lead into gold, our gift to others.

Having worked now with hundreds of women in my Mysterial programs, I have come to understand the collective nature of this pattern, which I call the Father wound. It lives in women as a sense that no matter how hard we try, we can't quite fit into the patriarchal worldview that emphasizes and values the rational mind over the intuitive, order over free flow, mind over body, power over versus power with. We learn to find our belonging, to fit in, by disappearing parts of our authentic selves into the unconscious. We collapse our sense of a true authority, grounded in our sufficiency, and look outward for how to do it "right" and thus find our love, safety, and belonging.

With Norma's guidance, I began to see that this deep pattern of seeking a sense of belonging with others and then having that shattered had very clear footprints back through the sands of the past. In my early years I had aligned with powerful, glamorous, often narcissistic others to feel like I belonged. This played out with being a father's daughter, in the guru-centric spiritual group I was a part of for over a decade, with my first husband, with business colleagues, and with David. I projected strength, brilliance, and power onto them and refused to see their negative or darker parts.

My own sense of power, autonomy, and self-reliance went into the shadows, and I accepted the reflected glory as I polished their stars. I sacrificed myself in order to be seen as a good global servant—to find my place in the world and make my contribution. This was my shadow at play. And I would choose not to see the shadows of those I had projected my blind loyalty onto—always positively reframing or rationalizing why they did what they did. In return I would belong, would feel safe and secure.

When I was younger, my father used to call me the "shit disturber" because I would see what was going on and actually name it—often not very skillfully. When this happened, he would squelch me and my message. The same pattern showed up in a spiritual community I was a part of for fifteen years. I was one of the early truth tellers to name the patriarchal shadows of the organization. The reprisal was swift and harsh: my friends and the community turned on me, and I was in essence "kicked out of the kingdom" for seeing the shadows. I learned that in order to conserve belonging, I would have to give up seeing what I saw.

As I worked through these past patterns with Norma, I explored what I had projected out onto others and the world. I began to see the parts of myself that I had not been ready to own—the good, the bad and the ugly. I took more responsibility for what I had created in my life and what had happened with David.

After several months of inner exploration, I identified eight patterns that I had projected onto David and others before him as themes throughout my life. After integrating the emotional material connected to each pattern, I then created "turnaround" awareness phrases to energize the parts of myself I needed to reclaim. Norma guided me to articulate these as my embodied rights. She also encouraged me to identify embodied experiences of where I was already bringing these new parts of myself online in my life.

I created little cards for each one of them, using collage and colored pencil drawings, and compiled them into a small, handmade book that sits on my altar. They are still powerful for me today.

Later, I discovered that the seeds for each of the eight Mysterial Meta-Capacities were held within the soil of my shadow projections, and as I did this work I could sense these capacities beginning to sprout and take root more deeply as my Mysterial way of being.

Transforming Shadow into Strength

1. *Shadow Projection:* Being self-centered and self-absorbed.

Embodied Right: I have the right to be centered in myself, to know my needs and meet them.

Embodied Experience: I began to make sure that I was taking my own needs into account alongside everyone else's when a complicated decision needed to be made. Often that meant holding the tension of opposites. When a good friend of David's suggested, a few weeks after he died, that I print the autobiography David had been working on, I unequivocally said, "Are you fucking kidding me? There are a few other things I have to take care of first!"

Mysterial Meta-Capacity Seed: Embracing Paradox

---

2. *Shadow Projection:* Being unreliable and abandoning.

Embodied Right: I have the right to walk away from people and situations that are not correct in order to move forward.

Embodied Experience: I did not sell our house to the people who gave the lowball offer; I fired David's estate accountant, who was neither honest nor reliable; and ended a business partnership that was not working for me.

Mysterial Meta-Capacity Seed: Unfolding the Emergent

---

3. *Shadow Projection:* Being withholding and sealed behind a wall.

Embodied Right: I have the right to hold on to my energy to protect and not deplete myself.

Embodied Experience: In my process to determine whether to take on the PR role, I realized I could not do it to save everyone else if it was not good for me as well. I was prepared to walk away. I let go of my immature heroic identity as I discerned, event by event, what I could and could not do.

Mysterial Meta-Capacity Seed: Energy Stewardship

---

4. *Shadow:* Doing whatever one wants without concern for others.

Embodied Right: I have the right to know my inner guidance, to trust it and to follow it, to know what I know and do what I must do.

Embodied Experience: I followed my intuition to know when I needed to enact certain rituals or follow the sense of timing in the cycle, even when others did not agree. I allowed myself to be led by inner and outer signals. (This came into play when I was taking on the stewardship of the property, planning David's memorial, performing the release of his ashes, selling the house, letting Emma go, and moving through the mammogram scare.)

Mysterial Meta-Capacity Seed: Multi-Dimensional Knowing

---

5. *Shadow Projection:* Being disingenuous—a split in how one appears and the reality of who they are.

Embodied Right: I have the right to choose an identity of power and sufficiency, even if it is not complete, and express it authentically.

Embodied Experience: Even though I felt shattered and vulnerable, I was also able to show up in powerful ways as I negotiated through the close of David's business and the management of his debts. I gave a keynote address at the Emerging Women conference only six months after his death and allowed my vulnerability to be my powerful presence there.

Mysterial Meta-Capacity Seed: Authentic Presence

---

6. *Shadow Projection:* Use of strong, brutal force.

Embodied Right: I have the right to use my life force to have a BIG impact in the world. The job is done!

Embodied Experience: I had to make some very difficult and important decisions with large consequences related to where I would live, the resources I would have, and the people I would work with. I was willing to do what had to be done—using my power wisely—to bring order into the chaos.

Mysterial Meta-Capacity Seed: Influencing System Resonance

---

7. *Shadow Projection:* Using others' energy and not returning it.

Embodied Right: I have a right to receive creative energy from others in a reciprocal flow so that we both feel special.

Embodied Experience: I shifted my pattern of being the overgiver who propped up others in order to profoundly receive all that was being offered to me by friends, family, community, and colleagues. My core friendships dramatically deepened in this new field of reciprocity.

Mysterial Meta-Capacity Seed: Generative Mutuality

---

8. *Shadow Projection:* Grandiosity and narcissism.

Embodied Right: I have the right to be seen and appreciated as a sovereign being.

Embodied Experience: I stepped out of David's shadow and showed up as the one who was able to deal with the difficult consequences of the life he had left. I also stood in the midst of the devastation without sinking into the shame of his suicide and everything I'd lost. My sovereignty was about how, instead of hiding, I found a way to be present without being destroyed myself. I connected more fully to the collective by landing more firmly in my own authority.

Mysterial Meta-Capacity Seed: Tending the Field

I share these shadow projections, embodied rights, and embodied experiences because I believe this is the invitation of transformation that is extended to us when grief and loss rips us open and our lives fall apart. It can be a powerful moment to closely examine the ways of being that may not have served us and do the work of facing hard truths about how we have been unconsciously living from our shadows. We can frantically try to shore up our lives and put all our energy into getting back to where we were before—clinging to the familiar rather than responding to the evolutionary impulse that is calling us forward—but not only is this a more painful approach that slows the healing process, it also often doesn't work.

The alternative path is to allow the light of our conscious awareness into the darker corners that the trauma or loss we've experienced has exposed. I discovered that the rebirth seed potential of the Mysterial Meta-Capacities was locked within my shadows, and when I did the humbling work of turning toward these split-off parts of myself, a profound transformation took place.

After months of work with Norma to make the darkness conscious, I was ready to return, symbolically, to the moment when I found David and everything changed. I was ready to claim the choice to step onto this savage soul path that I was walking. I asked Norma to bear witness to this threshold moment.

To begin, I visualized myself back on that night of January 3, before I found David's body. I saw myself standing in the field, darkness all around, the rain pelting down on my shoulders. I saw the hot tub ahead of me and the path I would take toward it. I saw the uncertain and grueling trail that I would need to follow on the other side of it. I had no sense of false bravado about my ability to do what would be asked of me if I walked toward that hot tub. I felt only humility.

I stood in the place where the invitation for this life-changing journey was still open, where a choice could be made, and I said, *Yes—I choose to step forward on this path even though I do not know if I have it in me to do what life will ask of me. Yes. I accept my destiny.*

And then I stepped forward over a threshold that I had made with a stick between two stools. I would make my path by walking— and maybe, with grace and guidance, I would eventually return to the Upper World, transformed through this deepest of all dives into Hades.

Chapter 16:

Marking the Path Back

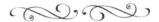

"I would love to live
Like a river flows,
Carried by the surprise
Of its own unfolding."

—JOHN O'DONOHUE

In the Kore/Persephone myth, the spring equinox is the time when the maiden Kore, having eaten the pomegranate seeds, emerges from her deep time in Hades. She brings the seeds of her embodied experience back to the Upper World and declares her Intention for the blossoming and fruit harvested from her descent.

This is a powerful moment in the story and in the cycle of a life. There are those times when we are dragged down into Hades by outer circumstances or by a deep soul calling. And there is a time to end that journey. There is an art to knowing when the descent has done its work and it is time to integrate the changes through the act of returning back into the world as the renewed self. Sometimes the dark becomes synonymous with connection to that which was lost and to leave the underworld seems like another unbearable level of letting go.

I had been using equinox and solstice punctuations in the annual calendar for decades as a time to do rituals. Now, as the spring equinox cycled around again each year, it was an opportunity for me to feel into where I actually was in my travels across the landscape of loss.

On the first spring equinox after David died in 2013, I heard from my real estate agent that an offer would be made on my house. It was a significant turn of events that would lead to a sale and make it possible for me to exit the hottest fires of Hades. But my time in the underworld was still far from complete.

At the end of the second year, on the spring equinox of 2014, I sat in a powerful circle with women from my Mysterial Crone Council—these were women who had gathered around me when I fell into the abyss and helped me to hold safe the seeds of our Mysterial work while everything else was breaking apart. We sat in Circle and spoke about what we each saw emerging. There was so much kindness and care in these times together. While my own vision was still eclipsed by my trauma and all that I needed to attend to in the present, I was so grateful to have their eyes to see what I still could not and to remind me of what might be possible.

The first two years were full of so much change in every area of my life. In my Mysterial work, it had become crystal clear that the women's leadership business that I had built over a decade had to transform. It was only three years earlier that I had taken on two business partners to expand and grow our work in the world. Now I knew that this structure was no longer correct—not only for me but also for my partners. Dissolving the partnership so that the business returned to me was the right next step, but what I would make of it next, if anything, was far from clear.

When we shifted the business back to me, I was not yet ready to do public programs. Slowly, I started to work in one-on-one coaching with women, guiding them through the Mysterial Sequence in an intimate journey. I had never done this before, as all of our research had been done in cohort programs. It was a potent opportunity for me to take the work deeply back into myself and refine it in ways that weren't possible in the larger programs.

The following year, on the equinox of 2015, there was a powerful new moon in Pisces, along with a total solar eclipse. The astrological influences were all about self-transformation, and I used this alignment of energies to consciously bring myself out into the Upper World. I had returned to completing the *The Way of the Mysterial Woman* manuscript with my coauthor Susan Cannon, we had just found a publisher, and the book was scheduled to launch in the following spring of 2016. It was time to begin my return to the world, and I used the equinox energy to do a public event.

Like many rituals that happened over the years, the astrological alignments for this gathering were uncanny. I wanted to hold the Mysterial Circle at a beautiful event space in Seattle, enchantingly decorated with strings of twinkling lights and equipped with a powerful sound system for dancing to the archetypal energies of The Mysterial Sequence—and I discovered that the only date they had available was on the equinox. How synchronous, I thought, that my own emergence would align with the mythic return of Persephone to the Upper World.

In the midst of so much uncertainty, I felt a powerful sense of reassurance when once again my own timing aligned with cycles so much larger than me. I felt the steady hand of a universal force greater than my own personal will on the rudder of my small vessel, which was bobbing up and down on the still-unsettled seas of my life. It was comforting to sense that I was not alone and that in the midst of the chaos I was on my way . . . and maybe even right on time.

On the evening of the event, I was nervous and excited to be returning to the world again and full of hope that I was indeed going to come through this trial by fire intact. There were sixty-five women present in this powerful experiential launch event, and I could tangibly feel the enthusiastic welcome back. I spoke about my underworld grab, the trials of my descent, the book I had finished with Susan, and my hope for the work ahead with women's awakening and leadership.

My close friends who had seen me through the days and months after David died were there by my side that evening, as were many of the women I had once trained and led through the Mysterial Sequence in the years before David's death. I felt like someone returning from the wars and being welcomed back into her rightful place in the community. It was a new beginning.

But I was still not fully out of Hades. It would take another year for me to come all the way up and out.

On the next spring equinox of 2016, a few months before my book would be published, I knew it was time to do a ritual that would acknowledge the threshold I was crossing over as I stepped into the outer-world realities of public speaking and launching programs that were on the horizon for after our book was published.

In some miracle of scheduling, almost all of the dear friends of my "trauma tribe"—those who had been closely with me from the beginning—were able to join me in this ritual process. Although I was clearly the one who had taken the deepest dive since David's death, everyone in this Circle had been pulled down with me into the gravitational force field of his suicide. It had deeply impacted us all, and I was hopeful that bearing witness to my emergence might also be a kind of return for them.

Antonia, my dear friend who had traveled with me to Maui, and her partner, Rob, who had found David's body, offered their home and land for this ritual process. It was across the street from our old estate, and yet very different: while our property was seventeen acres of wide-open views, their land and home were tucked sweetly into the forest. We shared the same lofty view down into a steep ravine and creek bed below, however, so their home held the energies of place I was seeking.

Tears spontaneously welled up in my eyes as I looked around at my twelve beloved friends, all gathered in the cozy living room, as a soft rain fell outside and the many candles Antonia had lit glowed everywhere around us.

I felt my heart cracking open as I said, "Thank you, my dearest friends, for coming to bear witness to my emergence today and to help me cross back from the Underworld and into the Upper World. I know that it is time now to ritually honor where I have been the past three years, and to symbolically call all of myself back so that I am ready to step into the world with our book and my work. And I also hope that participating in this ritual will be an opportunity for you, too, to call parts of yourself back home from the Underworld . . ."

I went on, telling them that I knew it was time to leave the dark night that had broken me open and reshaped everything about my inner and outer life, and yet I was also afraid that doing so might mean leaving David and the life I'd known and loved even further behind. I explained that I also understood that it was possible for me to continue to carry my love for David and all that we'd shared—not as a nostalgic longing for what was gone but as a fundamental part of my wholeness. I would need help, though, to make this transition.

Ritual is a powerful way to integrate the conscious and the unconscious. I wanted to access my confidence and step forward, and I knew that I needed to claim my own life and further release David, but my unconscious self was still not so sure. That was why I was so determined to perform this ritual and so grateful for the support of my friends.

I began the ritual by descending down into the ravine behind the house. Antonia, a shamanic practitioner, was my guide to lead me down and back again. I asked my friend Deborah, who had been with me since the first terrible night of trauma, to walk beside me as my soul sister. I asked David's dear friend Richard to stand in as David, walking with me and bearing witness to all that this journey, which his death had initiated, had been for me. I gave Richard my favorite rusty orange sweater of David's to wear, and as he put it on I felt David's energy arriving.

The community gathered at the top of the ravine and Antonia took her place at the edge. She was wearing a dark blue felt coat with a big hood, and as she dropped into her role as ritual guide she lifted her rattles to call in the Four Directions and shapeshifted before us into Hekate, the Crone goddess who guided Perspehone between the realms. And then with the sound of the rattles still ringing in the air, Antonia, Deborah, Richard, and I turned and left our friends in the Upper World as we traveled back in time and went down into the ravine.

In preparation for the ritual, I had identified the eight Embodied Rights that I was bringing out of Hades and had reflected on what I was ready to let go of in order to allow these seed commitments to blossom and fruit in this new phase of my life. I had written them on orange ribbons that were tied around eight young narcissus plants in their little green pots. It was the narcissus flower, a powerful symbol of rebirth and new beginnings, that Persephone was picking when the earth opened up and Hades emerged on his thundering chariot to drag her off into the underworld.

Deborah transported the small pots on a tray and as we journeyed down the muddy and slippery trail to the creek bed at the bottom, I stopped at various places and one by one left the eight narcissus plants with the bright orange ribbons along the trail. They would play their part later in the ritual.

A recent storm had left the trail badly eroded, and it was a tough journey down the steep, 400-foot embankment. Somehow that seemed just right—covered with mud and with my old knee injury reactivated, I felt the painful reality of the descent into and the climb out of the crater that David's death had left in my life over the last three years. This ritual process was a powerful symbolic echo of my actual experience.

When we finally arrived at the bottom of the ravine, the air was still and sacred. Moss trailed from the trees like ancient lace and the fecund scent of the earth hung in the air. The only sound was the creek's trickling water, the tops of the cedar trees rubbing against one another in the wind, and the occasional robin adding its lilting birdsong.

I was touched by the simplicity and emptiness of this place. It was a perfect mirror for the journey. Like the moment between the exhale and the inhale, everything seemed held in suspension—the path behind complete, the path ahead not yet chosen.

There was something profoundly beautiful about giving myself to this place in between; time itself fell away, and the silence was thick with presence. Into the quiet of this valley, I spoke aloud my Intention for the journey ahead, casting my vision out in front of me and onto the ground of the awaiting Upper World. I would need my future self on belay, pulling me up and out of this darkness.

"I am deeply rested into the Yin nectar sufficiency of my being as I stand visible and available to receive the women and abundance that are coming toward me. I am in generative, creative partnerships and held in the loving presence of a substantial man who sees me, meets me, loves me, plays with me, and is a true life partner."

Antonia channeled a powerful invocation when I was done and then—as we had done many times before, including when I released David from his stewardship of the land—we all said the Ho'oponopono Prayer before heading back:

> *I'm sorry.*
> *Please forgive me.*
> *Thank you.*
> *I love you.*

I knew the walk back up was going to be hard and my knee was already throbbing. Yet this, too, was so representative of the many mornings I'd woken up dreading the day and feeling uncertain of how I would make it through. I began by just placing one foot in front of the other. One step at a time.

"We make our path by walking," I said as I turned and took the first painful step up the slippery slope.

We stopped eight times on the way up, at each of the narcissus plants that I had left on the way down. Each time, I untied the ribbon and spoke to what I was leaving behind in the underworld and the seed of the new Embodied Right that I was opening to receive. When I was done, Deborah removed the ribbons from the narcissus and tied them one at a time around my arm. Beholding my growth was a powerful integrating move for me as I stood in the place in myself where I could actually see how far I had come since those devastating early days.

Step by step, we made our way up out of the ravine, slipping and sliding on the muddy trail, as I declared my Embodied Rights. My knee would hardly bend and each step felt like an enormous accomplishment. When we finally crested the top I could see in the distance my dear friends, waiting on the lawn with warm smiles.

Antonia stood tall in her shapeshifted way at the edge of the ravine, lifting the rattle up above her head and shaking it strongly to mark our exit from the darkness, as we completed our climb. I had asked my friend Dianne to step into the role of Demeter—the Mother Goddess who welcomed Kore back from her trip to the Underworld—and she was standing on the other side of a low arched doorway into the garden, a handful of freshly picked spring flowers in her hands.

But before I crossed under the arch and out into the welcoming arms of my friends, I invited Richard, who was standing in for David, to channel for me his words of blessing.

"Suzanne," he said. "I left you in a way that no one should ever be left. Everything that I could not face or handle you carried for me. You accepted the burden of my life choices. I simply did not have the strength or the will to continue on. You did. I thank you. I am so proud of you and all that you have accomplished. You have been wise in the midst of so many difficult decisions. You have been strong through one loss after the other and still able to keep the thread of your own work with women alive. You have been loving through this nightmare in ways that soothed the hearts of the many people whom I wounded. I'm sorry. Please forgive me. Thank you. I love you."

My whole body shook as Richard/David spoke to me and I received his love and blessing deep in my heart.

Richard then pulled off David's sweater and releasing his role, crossed out under the arch to return to his place as my dear friend and ally on this journey. Then Deborah crossed over the threshold, and I was alone.

Ultimately, although many dear friends had come with me on this journey in the last three years, I had found a new connection to my adult aloneness—one that was less a terrifying emptiness and more a fullness in the intimacy with myself.

I stood now in this fullness. A soft wind blew up from the ravine and I could feel its gentle breath nudging me over this last threshold. With a final bow to the journey itself—to all that it had been, to who I had become through it, and to the great mystery ahead—I crossed under the arch and into Dianne's loving arms and a joyous celebration with my community. I was ready now to welcome the new world that awaited me.

Chapter 17:

Mending a Broken Heart

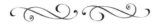

"Out of a great need
We are all holding hands
And climbing
Not loving is a letting go.
Listen, the terrain around here
Is far too dangerous for that."

—Hafiz

As I turned further into my new life and released David at the bottom of the ravine during the ritual, there was a very specific shift in my openness to the possibility of an intimate relationship again.

A year earlier, I was attending the re-commitment marriage ceremony of my dear friends when Rick—the same Rick who as a forensic accountant had helped me navigate through the first months of all the chaos and confusion of David's financial affairs—asked to speak to me alone.

I immediately thought that he had information for me about some financial peril that I needed to prepare for. The estate had closed in court a few years earlier and because I had sold the house at a good price, some of his family and friends who had secured credit received their funds, and I received the Award of Family Support funds to begin my life again. Although I had been told that I was not responsible for David's enormous debt, I still lived with the constant fear that some new nefarious dealing of his would be discovered.

Instead of news of financial doom, however, Rick said, "I have an idea I want to pass by you. I know you might not be ready for this, but I just thought that I would ask. I have a client who has become a friend. He has suggested that he, Julia, and I go out to dinner one night, and I thought you could be a fourth."

This wouldn't be a date, he assured me, this would just be a fun night out.

"He is a skier and a biker, a neuroscientist toxicologist, and he has his own company," Rick said. For the clincher, he added, "And he speaks French and lives in your neighborhood."

My reaction was swift and direct: "I am just not ready for dating or meeting men yet. But thanks for thinking of me."

But Rick didn't let it go there. "Well, just talk to Julia about it and see what she says," he said.

After a pep talk from Julia, who encouraged me to use the opportunity as a way to take a simple step forward, I reluctantly agreed to go.

In the journey back into the relational world after the loss of a beloved partner, there are particular thresholds that must be acknowledged and crossed carefully. This was one of them. To choose to go out for dinner with a new man and my friends was to admit that there was some part of me open to beginning with another partner one day. This meant stepping further away from the me who was committed to David, whom I'd believed to be my life partner.

I looked Richard up online and the photo I found showed a man with a beard who didn't look like my type. It made it easier to go out to dinner knowing that he would be "just a guy"; this would just be a ritual of crossing over the threshold toward my desired future, I decided, not a true potential match.

Sitting in my car outside of the restaurant—all dressed up and feeling a sense of nervous excitement, anger, and dread all mixed together—I called Dianne.

The moment she answered, I broke down crying. "I can't do this. I am so fucking angry with David that I have to do this . . . dress up and start over again from scratch. I want him to be here. I want to be going out to dinner with him!"

Dianne's soothing voice gently urged me forward. "I know, sister. This is not easy. But you are strong. And you can do this. Remember what you always say, 'You make your path by walking.' This is just the next step forward. And you can do it."

Richard was the last to arrive. Rick and Julia and I were waiting for him at our table when I noticed a handsome—beardless—man walk into the front lobby. I recognized him in some strange energetic way and said to myself, *It's a good thing that isn't the guy or I would be in trouble!*

But then I saw the hostess point over toward our table and a wave of anxiety washed over me.

I had chosen to sit far away from him—asking Julia to sit opposite the "other man"—so he wouldn't think it was a date. That evening, there were lots of fun and lively stories around the table about skiing and biking adventures, but it was clear to me that Richard and I did not live in the same universe. I oriented more toward the psychospiritual dimensions of existence and the human potential movement, whereas he oriented more to the linear, scientific, and practical realms. It had not yet occurred to me that a man with these qualities could be exactly the healing balance needed after the trauma of being left by my spiritually bypassing husband.

I was surprised at the end of the night, as we all stood together getting ready to leave, that I felt so comfortable and at ease in Richard's energy. My body seemed to settle in the presence of this man with whom I was sure I did not have enough in common.

In fact it took two years and several steps backward before this initial sense of soul connection would show itself more fully. Richard had women to date, freedom after his divorce to experience, and himself to discover. I had a book to launch, a company to grow, and a heart to heal.

During that time, since Richard and I lived a few blocks from one another, we got into the habit of meeting every few months at our local wine bar, Bottlehouse, for a drink. It was always interesting and fun and I enjoyed the safe, flirtatious energy between us. At our first rendezvous there I said to him very directly, "Just to be clear, I want you to know that this is not a date; I am not interested in dating. But I would love to become a friend." I imagine that my unconscious already sensed he was in my future and I knew that I was not ready yet.

There was one extraordinary synchronicity that occurred during the first year of our getting to know one another as friends. After a few years of keeping all the beautiful antiques that couldn't fit in my small house in a storage unit, I realized that I wasn't going to be moving into a larger home anytime soon, and the cost of storing the heavy teak pieces no longer made sense; I would have to let go of these beauties.

I had been told earlier by the psychic Lynn Austin that David was going to send someone to buy a large part of my collection. So I set out to find that person. I assumed this someone would be an antique dealer, so I began by contacting all of the people I knew who sold Javanese antique furniture to see if they wanted to buy anything. When nobody came forward, I found someone with a pop-up store in Seattle and was able to get my furniture out of storage and show it there for three months.

One day during this period, Richard came over to my house for a glass of wine, and when he saw all my antique pieces he instantly fell in love with them. He was in the middle of a home renovation and thought this style would fit well with his newly emerging decor. The next day he went to the pop-up in Ballard and bought most of the collection.

My friendship with Richard continued growing, and about four years after David died, eighteen months after meeting Richard, and several months after my equinox ritual, I began to feel something opening in me that told me I might be ready to meet someone again.

To give a little more energy to this seed idea, I created a vision board of collaged images representing everything that I was intending for the year ahead, a whole section of which was images with a partner—relaxing comfortably at home, skiing, biking, and traveling the world.

A few months later, right before Valentine's Day, Richard and I were sitting having dinner together at the bar of a local restaurant, and in the middle of our conversation he simply leaned over and kissed me.

I was stunned into silence. My body felt frozen, and yet my heart was open—a strange sensation.

When a few days later we shared a deeper kiss, the full impact of this opening hit. Without any warning, a huge wave of grief moved through me; I started to sob and my body began to shake.

Richard was so kind and compassionate. He of course had no idea what had just happened, but he knew enough to hold me in his strong arms until the wave had moved through. Later I came to understand the way trauma is released by the body. We think we get over things, but the truth is that the body keeps track of everything, and it heals in its own way and in its own time.

Bessel van der Kolk, one of the world's foremost experts on trauma, describes in his best-selling book *The Body Keeps the Score* how people who have experienced trauma live in a kind of dual reality—"the reality of a relatively secure and predictable present that lives side by side with a ruinous, ever-present past."

The last time I had shared an intimate kiss like this was with David the morning of the day he died. I had forgotten it. Now, kissing Richard, it suddenly came rushing back through me, and I realized in that moment that David's kiss had been his goodbye. I'd thought at the time that it was goodbye until later that night, but he'd known that it was goodbye for this lifetime.

When you lose a beloved partner, there are layers of healing that cannot occur until you open your heart again to another. When Richard and I started entering into the intimate parts of our relationship and the heat of passion reentered my system, the frozen parts of me—the grief, the fear, the anger, and the love—all started to thaw. It was messy and heartbreaking. At some moments it was so sweet to feel love again, and at others, when I experienced Richard not showing up in the ways I needed him to, I fell into the trauma of the loss again and was consumed by great waves of despair.

While Richard certainly had his own work to do as he reentered the relational sphere after his divorce, I knew that the intensity of my response to his lack of presence was way out of proportion to the events that occurred. My attachment system needed healing.

Slowly but surely, with the help of my therapist, Erica, as well as my friend Dianne and Richard himself, I began to find a very new ground in our relationship.

The total solar eclipse of August 21, 2017, dubbed the "Great American Eclipse" by the media, marked a significant step forward for me and for my relationship with Richard.

I was on Lopez Island up in the beautiful San Juan Islands in the Pacific Northwest for a week of working on this book. Before I would dive into that, Richard came to join me for a weekend. I was staying in my friend Stephen's small cottage where the expansive, south-facing view out across an open field was perfect for this celestial convergence of earth, moon, and sun.

It was the new moon again, of course. My friend. My guide during the darkest days of the first year. She was going to cross over the face of the blazing sun and for a short period of time—only twenty seconds—would block the solar force out completely.

I had brought eclipse glasses that would allow us to watch the phenomenon directly. We put them on and watched as the moon—her dark face full toward the earth—crept slowly over the top right corner of the sun, removing at first just the smallest semi-circle of solar brightness.

It took until she was about halfway across to really notice the shift in the quality of the light. Although it was still a sunny morning, something from the color spectrum was missing; everything was a little less bright and glowing. It was as though someone had turned the thermostat down by one-third and the heat that would normally warm the skin was gone, leaving a chill down to the bone.

There was an eerie quality in the air—and emptiness of sound. As we approached 92 percent coverage, the birds went completely silent. They stayed like this for five to ten minutes, until the moon started to move off of the sun.

As the moon was leaving the sun's face, it spontaneously occurred to me to read the letter David had written to me before he took his life to the man to whom I was now opening mine. I had it with me as part of the preparation for my writing week.

I had wondered if at some point, when my heart opened again to another man, I would read this letter to him. I imagined that I would want that new man to know not only the me that had been left in such a horrific manner but also the me who had been loved deeply. Maybe I would also want him to know that I was not responsible for David's death to ease my guilt and shame about it all. And maybe I also would want the man to whom I was opening my heart to know David's heart as well. To hear his suffering. To sense his soul turmoil. To not reduce him to a monster.

It had been so hard for me to reckon with the man who loved my broken places into wholeness and then left me in a way that put that wholeness to the test. How could anyone else make sense of this if I was only just beginning to myself? But maybe reading his letter could help.

It turned out that I read the letter to Richard just after the peak moment of the solar eclipse. Later, it occurred to me that this was a kind of celestial perfection that I could not have orchestrated had I tried. The solar eclipse was like a metaphor for the whole experience of the previous four years. The dark face of the moon draining away the heat and light from the sun was just like what I'd felt when David died: A darkness I could never have imagined laying itself over the natural joy and aliveness in my heart. All the heat gone. All the bright colors drained of their vibrancy. The world gray and lifeless.

I read his first word to me—*Honeybun*—and it hung in the air for many moments as tears streamed down my face.

This was our pet word for one another. I am not sure how it started exactly, but David loved to call me this. It said so much. He didn't use this word for anyone else—he never had even imagined that he would have someone in his life whom he could call honeybun—and in this simple word was all of his love for me.

I continued on, reading the poignant words of a man who loved me fully but had lost faith in himself, who was ashamed to be leaving me in this way, and who asked me if I could, in time, find a way to forgive him. I read the words of a broken man who shared his faith in me and all that I would bring into the world.

As I read the final words of his letter, the warmth of the eclipsed sun started to return to our landscape.

And if in fact
I have another life to live
I hope and pray that we will
meet again & I can begin
to embody & reciprocate all
the love that you have
showered on me.
In undying &
eternal love,
David

It was a vulnerable moment to expose myself, David, and our "we space" to Richard. And it was a lot for him to take in. But he did. When I was done, he reached out his hands for mine and then took me into his strong arms.

It has been five years now of Richard and I deepening our relationship together, and I am so grateful that we have both been willing to keep growing up and showing up with one another. I have a deepening sense of belonging in our relationship and at the same time I feel my own adult aloneness as a profound belonging to myself. I do not take relationships for granted at this point in my life and feel enormously lucky to have found someone with Richard's deeply open heart, growth mindset, and willingness to walk with me over the hot coals of my healing and reentry into the world.

I have learned to love again not in spite of my wounded heart but because of it. The loss that brought me to my knees is the same loss that has carried me through to a more vulnerable, permeable, loving, and lovable self. I am making my path by walking slowly toward love again.

Chapter 18:

The Ground of a New Life

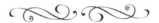

*"The most beautiful people we have known
are those who have known defeat, known suffering,
known struggle, known loss, and have found their way
out of the depths. These persons have an appreciation,
a sensitivity, and an understanding of life that fills
them with compassion, gentleness, and a deep loving
concern. Beautiful people do not just happen."*

—Elisabeth Kübler-Ross

*Have I arrived on the shore of a new life?
Maybe the boatman rode me in on a quiet wave
in the dark of night
and humbly left me on the empty strand.
No trumpets, no cosmic moon alignments,
no obvious thresholds crossed.
What if this simple arriving is enough?
A toehold,
a few grains of sand beneath my feet,
enough for my first steps forward.*

I have waited for some sign that this difficult passage is over.
The dark nights,
the terrors unspoken,
the nose to the grindstone,
the Sisyphean pushing of the stone uphill,
the endless uncertainty.
That it is done.
The seeds counted,
the sheaves of grain piled neatly,
the sacrifices made on the altar of loss.

What if this is all that must be given now?
The cup turned back over
wider and deeper for its journey
open to be filled again.

What if there is no grand resurrection?
Instead, the simple act of
walking along this new shore
uncertain, innocent, hopeful.

Leaving footprints in the wet sand,
saying I have come from somewhere,
I am going somewhere,
And I am here now.

I find myself standing now on very new ground in my life. How did I get here? There was no straight line possible from the life I had before David died to the life I have now. Everything was dismantled—my home, my business, my primary relationships, my community—and I worked in a very emergent way to be where I am today. I walked step by intuitive step for many years, until one day I turned around and saw the coherence and beauty of the path that I had been on. The Mysterial Meta-Capacities were my lived experience now . . . not in spite of my traumatic journey but because of the intensity of the process.

If we have been lucky enough, if we have been willing enough to face the uncertainty and let go of the path that is no longer ours to walk, we will find the way forward that is untrodden by anyone else and uniquely ours. For this to happen, we must learn to trust ourselves and lean into the winds of our fate.

One of the first things I needed to learn as I set off on this new path was how to manage all the anxiety and fear that would arise during the day and especially at night. I knew that the freedom I was seeking as I built my new life would require me to work with fear in ways that I had never done before.

My nervous system, too, had to be recalibrated after David died. At first the anxiety was overwhelming. I knew how to metabolize fear to some extent, having done this for many years in my programs. But this was way over my threshold for integration. I was barely eating. I have a memory of times with my friend Sharleen when she and I would sit together, having dinner with other friends, and every now and again she would take a forkful of food and pop it in my mouth. I was like a baby bird who needed this kind of tending. I was also not sleeping well. The nights were full of terror and grief and my body could not settle. I tried all my techniques for breathing through the fears, being with the feelings, etc., and it was just too much.

I had never taken any kind of sleep or anxiety medication and I had the opinion that they were not necessary—that I could deal with my fear on my own. But as the days of no sleep accumulated, it became clear this was not the case. I was exhausted; and because of that exhaustion, I had less capacity to face all that needed my full presence. Susan, a friend who had only a year earlier lost her husband in a tragic rock climbing accident and was also into all things natural, urged me to get some help.

So I crossed over another threshold and got the help of a sleep medicine. I finally slept. My body was deeply grateful. And it gave me the healing time I needed to be able to be with all the feelings that arose during the day.

During times of enormous uncertainty and change, we need the capacity to slide into the dark—to let go and to belong to the dreamlands. Even now, when I am working with women in my programs who have gone through enormous transitions or loss, one of the first questions I always ask is, "Are you sleeping?" If not, that is where we must begin.

Every day following David's death was an opportunity to be kind and compassionate to the self that was going through this enormous trauma. I began to treat myself more and more like a precious being. I became my own best friend. Almost daily, I would use a simple somatic practice that we teach in our programs and that is grounded in Dr. Kristin Neff's excellent research on self-compassion. Holding my hands gently over my heart, I would say:

Suzanne, this is a moment of suffering. This is hard right now.
We all struggle in our lives—I am not alone.
May I hold myself with tenderness in this moment.
May I be kind to myself in this moment.
May I be compassionate with myself in this moment.

Another way I took care of myself through the intensity of those first six months was through weekly sessions with Catherine, a craniosacral practitioner. I would arrive in her small studio broken and drained of substance, and over the course of that hour the well of my being would refill with sweet nectar. Having been through her own life traumas, Catherine would not allow me to pay for the sessions, although I was eventually able to give her some beautiful antique stones for her garden.

Susan, my massage therapist who recommended the sleep aid early on, was another regular healing sanctuary for my battered being. And weekly sessions with Erica, my loving and skilled therapist, were a core component of my healing journey. It was in her safe office where I could really let myself fall apart and come together again. She slowly walked me back into my life and even came to my home before I left to bear witness to what I was releasing. Without these gifts from these women healers, I don't know how I would have made it through my darkest days.

Sometimes, when the waves of terror were more than I could manage on my own, I called Sharleen, who had volunteered to be on my Support Call team. I remember one particularly poignant time after I had moved into Seattle. It was a Sunday afternoon, and I had gone out to University Village Mall to do some shopping, thinking that I was ready for the world. But I was not. Walking around in the midst of others doing their normal everyday things—couples holding hands, people laughing, children playing—it was all too much. Suddenly a huge wave of grief and terror moved through me and I was totally caught off guard by a panic attack.

I staggered to a bench, sat down, and called Sharleen. I burst into tears once I heard her kind voice and I let the wave move through me.

"Feel the solid bench you're sitting on," she coached me gently. "Bring your breath down into your belly. You're okay. I'm right here. I'm so sorry, sweetie, that it's so hard. You just aren't ready for this yet. It's okay."

She stayed on the phone with me until I was back in my car and heading home.

———

As I moved further and further back into the world over the next many years, I continued to cultivate my capacity to transform fear from overwhelm to aliveness. I became a dedicated fear researcher and I was also the specimen in the petri dish. I had lost everything that mattered most to me and could identify with all the fears on the rungs of Maslow's hierarchy of needs. I was afraid that I would not have a roof over my head, food to eat, a livelihood; I was afraid I would never have a relationship again; I was afraid of the consequences of important decisions I was making, afraid of disappointing others, afraid that I wouldn't fulfill my destiny on earth. Fear was a constant in my life.

As often as I could when one of these primal fears arose, I would slow myself down. I would bring myself back into the present moment by asking, *Is there any life or death threat in this moment?* I would quiet my mind, let the stories go, and feel my feet on the floor. And I would say to myself, *In this moment I am safe, I have a beautiful home, I have food, I am loved, I have my health. I am okay.*

I would often awaken with an intense flood of panic in the middle of the night. The feelings were accompanied by a hot flash and hormones rushing through my body. I tried many different things to get through these moments, but ultimately the most powerful was to imagine myself riding the waves of anxiety on a surfboard: I would see myself on the wave as it moved, keep my mind quiet, and breathe deeply until I landed on the beach. Although excruciating in the moment, usually it did not take long for the feelings to settle once I had turned toward them.

The late Vietnamese spiritual teacher Thich Nhat Hanh powerfully said, "The only way to ease our fear and be truly happy is to acknowledge our fear and look deeply at its source. Instead of trying to escape from our fear, we can invite it up to our awareness and look at it clearly and deeply."

As it turned out, my studying of fear with such depth and intensity as I made my way into my new life was also powerful training for living in the uncertain times of today. There is enormous collective anxiety in the world right now relative to the pandemic, economic instability, geopolitical intensities, climate crisis, social upheaval, and more. When you add in the personal factors in our own lives, it is a lot to handle.

As individuals who are choosing to be on the edge of evolution, shaping a new world through our consciousness and actions, we will have to learn to work with fear and uncertainty. If we try to avoid the discomfort in our bodies when fear arises we will find that our worlds grow smaller and smaller. Freedom and authentic self-expression are possible when we do the very thing that our conditioned mind does not want us to do . . . and that is to turn toward the fears.

I was told a story once when I was in South Africa—a teaching fable that the elders used to encourage their youth to go toward their fear—that has stuck with me. When the lions are hunting across the plains, they have a tactic that involves the oldest male lion with the loudest roar going into the long grass on one side of a trail. On the other side of the trail, the younger male lions quietly wait in the grass. When a herd of roaming springbok antelope passes by, the old male lion lets out a mighty roar. Naturally, the springboks run in the opposite direction, where the waiting lions catch their prey.

The moral of the story?

Run toward the roar! Run toward your fear!

Turning toward the fear that is deep within the well of loss was the invitation of my own traumatic journey and is the invitation of these times. This is very different from trying to power through fear—becoming fearless—without acknowledging what you are feeling or overidentifying with the emotion and shutting down.

I am not saying that there aren't times to listen to the fear response; when things are genuinely dangerous, this is what keeps us safe. But far too often our habitual response is based on something that is no longer true; the issue or situation is not actually life and death, even though that is what the body and conditioned mind would like to tell us.

Things are not going to get easier or more certain anytime soon. We are being asked to grow the capacity to transform our outdated fear responses and experience the freedom that exists on the other side. This is where the eight Mysterial Meta-Capacities come in— they are the seed code for this new way of being and a new world.

Over the last five years, using our new online format, the Mysterial Woman pathway and program has carried many women through the healing of the developmental traumas of their lives and lifted them into profoundly new ways of being, doing, and leading. When the world order ground to a halt in 2020 with COVID-19, we had many of the capacities coming online already to respond to the fear, confusion, and suffering that we and many others were experiencing.

In a way that I could never have imagined, my own journey of loss and resilience equipped me to be a guide for women during these enormously disruptive times—assisting them to let the breaking-open be a breaking-*through*—to a new level of consciousness and leadership capacity. When all those years ago in Bali I said,

"Yes I will help to midwife the Divine Feminine on earth," I could never have foreseen the route that would bring me to this moment.

Walking my path through the darkness, I learned to see that we are all beautiful, vast beings living in a beautiful and vast universe. And our human suffering is part of our vastness. There were times when I felt so porous to the poignancy of this that I could well up at almost anything: an old man sitting on a bus stop bench dressed in his Sunday best holding a bouquet of flowers, simple human decency, a young woman in a wheelchair struggling to get out of her car, soulful works of art or music. It was something about knowing the preciousness of life—knowing how we would all eventually lose it and everything we love—that broke me open and into the world.

I learned very personally when trauma hit my life that I could either numb out, flee, stay stuck and feel hopeless, or I could recognize this suffering as part of my human experience and stay fully present in the transformative fire.

Our challenge, then, is to do the very thing that our conscious mind has been working hard to prevent. We have to turn toward the feelings that were unbearable when we were younger and that can still seem unbearable now. We will need to find the guides who can take us down into the shadow lands as we do in our Mysterial work with women. There is a basic immunity to change built into our psyche and it will take something to disrupt the homeostatic seeking system. In the resources section, you will find a simple, five-step process you can use to further your exploration of turning toward and transforming intense feelings.

We find our inner vastness through these simple acts of liberating ourselves from our old patterns of thinking, feeling, and sensing. And it is this expansive consciousness that we need now—not only to hold the complexity of our own personal worlds in a very new way, but also to hold the challenging factors in our global, interconnected world.

Bitterness, hopelessness, and despair were not options that I chose during the devastation of my life—and they are not options that I want us to choose now.

To choose better options, we will need the Mysterial Meta-Capacities that I test-drove over the course of my own traumatic and transformational journey. This advanced Mysterial inner operating system is coming in now for the first time as an evolutionary move forward for our species. We need these crucial capacities to take on the challenges of a society that is outstripping what we constructed with our earlier meaning-making consciousness. The old patriarchal codes that have shaped identity for millennia need to be updated with healthier ways of being and doing that combine our Feminine and the Masculine strengths into an unprecedented inner alchemy.

Accepting that the personal and collective traumas that we experience are our connection to the great evolutionary upgrade, rather than the thing we have to get past in order to really make our contribution to the world, is a powerful shift.

We are needed now, both to serve as the calm waters in these fiery times and also to be the courageous shape-shifters birthing a new world order. Let your breaking open be the liberation of your hidden wholeness. The future is unwritten, waiting for you to inscribe your legacy across the heavens and manifest it on this beautiful earth as you make your path by walking.

A Mythic Journey

Part IV

With her dearest friends at her side, the queen set off with only the clothes on her back to begin again.

Outside the peaceful island she'd shared with her king, life was hard. She journeyed many moons through the dark forest, walking steadily but with no sure sense of direction. Her cup was empty and there was little that could fill her broken heart. Yet as she walked her lonely path she remained connected to a hidden wholeness and a deep inner faith that everything was unfolding as it should. She did not resist her destiny. Head held high, she walked on into the world.

Eventually she grew lighter on her feet and her eyes adjusted to the darkness. She made her path by walking. One step after another, she began to heal, and women who came to her small cottage in the woods to sit with her began to heal also. Soon, word of her healing powers spread around the land, and her voice grew stronger.

Over time her heart began to open and she fell in love with a learned man of science whose heart had also been broken. Unlike her king, when the new man's life had fallen apart he'd worked to build solid foundations in his life and grown stronger, and he was now awakening to his dreams. They healed each other's hearts, growing stronger in themselves and together.

As the years passed her memories faded and she began to wonder if she had ever truly been a queen in an otherworldly domain or whether it had all been just a dream.

And then one day, on the spring equinox, she had a powerful vision. She was shown that she had been sent by the goddess as a High Priestess to guide women home to themselves—but in order to do that she would first need to be initiated, learn to see in the dark, and remember herself.

Suddenly she saw around her the magical kingdom shimmering in the air, and she realized that she now stood on the solid ground of her own true home.

Epilogue

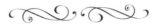

"We shall not cease from exploration
And the end of all our exploring
Will be to arrive where we started
And know the place for the first time."

—T.S. ELIOT

These last nine years since I was ripped from the fabric of belonging that I shared with David have been a profound journey into finally belonging to myself, and to the interconnected web of life. As I was pulling together my first draft manuscript for this book in March 2021 to send to my editor, I took a week to return to Vashon Island to write. I rented the Belle Baldwin cottage at my beloved Fern Cove, where so many threads of my life story converged so many years ago.

Fern Cove. It was the place that drew me to Vashon in the beginning—the sacred inlet that was one of the only freshwater salmon spawning rivers in all of Puget Sound, unobstructed from the mouth up to the creek head. I loved this cove from the moment my first husband and I happened upon it; so enchanted were we by its complex beauty, we bought a house just down the beach from it.

It is a place where the steady flow of fresh water meets the turning and tumbling of the saltwater tides. Where golden marsh grasses meet whip-like, dark rust kelp pulled onto the shore by the strong currents. Where gurgling sounds of the creek mix with the ocean waves crashing in against the beach, along with seagulls cawing, shore birds singing, ducks quacking, and geese announcing their arrival in long honks as they glide into the cove in the early evening.

When I first moved to Vashon I became a volunteer Salmon Stalker, which meant I was charged with walking down from my house with a clipboard every three days to keep track of the number of salmon I saw heading up the creek to spawn and die. I didn't see many, but the ones that I did see were an inspiration. Those old, mottled-gray, battle-scarred warriors swam upstream—slowly, but with determination—against the current. They had lived a long and hard life out there in the sea, and pure instinct was calling them back to this very creek, where they were born, to spawn and then, having passed their gift to the next generation, die.

It was always so poignant to me to witness these elders returning home. My father, with whom I had a very challenging relationship, was one of the world's top Atlantic salmon scientists, and it was not until I moved here that I understood his fascination with this fish. My deepening connection to them became a way for my father and me to find a new place of meeting in his later years.

It was also a place that David and I used to walk to on a regular basis, as it was just down the hill from our home. We would pack up our appetizers in a picnic basket, find our spot on the sandy beach, and sit quietly, watching the jewel-like sunsets. I learned from someone who saw him on the late afternoon of the day he died that they saw him walking to Fern Cove. I imagine it was the place that David chose for some of his last moments in this world. A final goodbye, perhaps, the bright sun of his own life about to go down forever. It was also the place where I released his ashes in a poignant ceremony at sunset with a small group of family and friends a year after he died.

And now I was back at Fern Cove, writing this book. The third day into my writing retreat I went out running in the early morning and made a trip to David's old boathouse/teahouse just down the beach from where I was staying. I remembered the first time I walked down the beach from my house to this little boathouse to meet David for tea. It was still as rustic and beautiful in its simplicity as when I had first visited.

The morning light was just starting to turn the landscape from gray to color as I reached the beachfront. My heart was touched to see this place, looking exactly as we had left it so many years before. It was not a feeling of nostalgia so much as it was a recognition of something that seemed to have stayed the same when everything else in my life had so dramatically changed.

I took a photo and just after snapping it, I somehow lost my footing. The ground seemed to shift beneath me, and I slid uncontrollably down a muddy slope and dropped five feet off the seawall onto the rocky beach below.

After the initial shock, the inevitable pain seared through my body. I'd suffered a very bad injury to my right ankle and was on my own, sitting on the beach.

I limped out to the main road, thinking that perhaps I would be able to walk home. I was clearly in shock, however, and it soon became evident that I wasn't going to go any farther. There were so many strange echoes in this moment of when I'd had the ground abruptly pulled out from under me when David took his life: one moment I was upright, in the life that I loved, and the next I was on a slippery slope, heading down, down, down, and landing with a crash, shattered on the rugged shore of a new and unwanted life.

⁓

I called my dear friends to help and Rob—who was with me on that first night, who found David and who held me then when I could not walk—was my hero again, delivering me this time back to my Airbnb. And while I was confined there with my injured ankle, my dear friends Dianne and Richard, who now lived on Vashon and who had walked with me along the difficult trail of rebuilding my life, came down to visit and spend cozy evenings with me, like we had done so many times in the years after David died.

There were other parallels with my past as well: my partner, Richard, was away at the time and it took a while to track him down, mirroring the pace of our meeting and slow connection years after my initial trauma.

So there I was at Fern Cove, mostly by myself writing and very much in my "adult aloneness"—not lonely but with myself in a very new way. I was there for me. Time seemed to slow down and I felt a kind of peace. Nowhere to go, nothing I could do but write and watch the sandpipers skitter back and forther in the mud, sit by the salmon-spawning creek and remember my father, and perch on a beach log at sunset and remember my David.

When I returned to Seattle a few days later, I felt like I had crossed over some kind of important threshold with the injury and the integrative time afterward, which had allowed me to weave together so many threads of my life that had come through Fern Cove. I scheduled an appointment to see a physician about my ankle, and the night before I went I had a powerful dream in which I was told that I had a broken tibia. As I was still able to put weight on my ankle, I was quite sure that my leg wasn't broken, but I tucked that information away inside—and when the doctor suggested it was just a bad sprain and I didn't need an x-ray, I insisted that I get one.

Sure enough, there was a break. To be precise, the medial malleolus, which is in fact the bump on the ankle at the end of the tibia, was broken.

In an extrodinary synchronicity, the ankle surgeon, the first person I could get in to see quickly, was the same doctor who had missed a broken foot diagnosis several years earlier. At the time I had asked for an x-ray of my foot, as I sensed it was broken, but in that arrogant doctor way he had said I didn't need one. I'd allowed his expertise to sway me until I'd gotten another opinion two weeks later, this time from a female physician who'd agreed to an x-ray and immediately found that my foot was indeed broken.

This time when I met with the male ankle surgeon I felt in full control of myself and was clear that I wanted to see if I could heal this fracture without surgery. As a surgeon he was naturally oriented toward operating, but when he fully examined the bone and saw that it was possible it could knit back together on its own if I got off of it totally, he agreed to explore that option. When I asked if he would hold with me a vision of a totally healed bone, he said that he had recently listened to an episode of an NPR radio show called *Hidden Brain* from which he had learned about the power of visualization and the possibility of mind influencing matter. He agreed to hold a positive intention for healing and gave me a week to see if the bone would start knitting together.

I kicked into high gear with bone healing supplements and various other healing modalaties. I even printed out a copy of my x-ray and, using a white pastel crayon, colored in the vast space in the crack on the medial malleolus and put the image on my altar to focus my intention. After one day on crutches going up and down stairs, moving around my house, and traveling between my house and my office studio in the backyard just about killed me, I did some googling and found a peg-leg like apparatus called the iWalk that I could strap to my leg and move about on with relative ease. I could do this.

In the first week's x-ray appointment, the doctor was stunned by the bone growth and declared that I would not need surgery if healing continued at that speed. I saw him every two weeks after that, and each time he would say that he had never seen anything like this before and to keep doing whatever I was doing.

My leg healed well and I am stronger than ever as a result of the PT and strengthening exercises I did afterward. Sometimes I can feel a throb deep in the ankle that reminds me of the break, but I accept that the pain is just part of what it is to be alive in this human body.

This whole experience felt like a mini-recapitulation of my eight-year journey after David's death. The person I have become through the trauma and loss is also stronger, more resilient, more compassionate, kinder to herself, and more loving with others. And there are also times when I feel the ache deep down in my bones for the love that I had with David, for what was between us and what might have been. And I recognize that this, too, is just what it means to be fully in this human life—daring to love with all your heart and willing to lose what you think you cannot live without.

And so I offer to you, my reader, as you go through your own disorienting, distressing, and difficult moments, one final wish—that you will do the only thing you can do, and know it is enough; that you will make your path by walking through the shattering of all your former selves, compelled, like the salmon, to return to an inner place of hidden wholeness that you may one day simply call home.

Resources

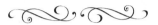

To understand more about the archetypal pathway for awakening the eight Mysterial Meta-Capacities that I write about in this book, please read my first book, *The Way of the Mysterial Woman: Upgrading How You Live, Love, and Lead,* co-authored with Dr. Susan Cannon. In it you will find the results of our research and compelling personal case stories of women who have done the inner work to liberate themselves to a whole new level of consciousness and leadership capacity. You will also find many powerful practices to help you awaken all the Feminine and Masculine strengths that accelerate the cultivation of the Mysterial Meta-Capacities.

The Mysterial Woman

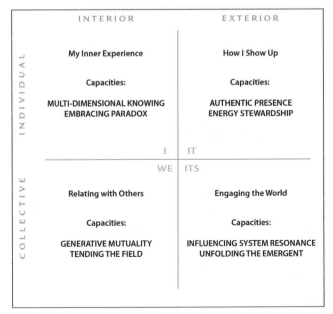

Morning Flow Practices

When you are walking the path of trauma or loss, how you enter into your day dramatically conditions the quality of your experience during the day. When David died, I already had a set of morning practices in place that I had been using for years, and they were essential to orient my consciousness when I would awake into the despair of my life. Although it will require planning ahead, and perhaps getting up earlier, the investment in yourself first thing in the morning is well worth it.

Ideally you would do all these practices sequentially.

1. Morning Pages

Morning pages, an idea borrowed from the work of Julia Cameron in *The Artist's Way*, is a stream-of-consciousness form of journaling that, with practice, leads to a stronger and clearer sense of self. These pages are a trail that you follow into your own inner landscape, where you have the potential to connect with the silent parts of yourself. They are a means to really let yourself feel what you feel, think what you think, and sense what you sense so that you do not drag all the unconscious material with you into the day. It can be very cathartic to let yourself express the messiness of the moment without trying to make it pretty or reframe it.

The process itself is very simple: First thing in the morning, find a comfortable place and write three pages (or write for fifteen minutes, whichever comes first), of longhand, strictly stream-of-consciousness writing. You might consider doing them in bed if the conditions are suitable. You really want to make sure you do morning pages before your mind gets a chance to gear up for the day.

What is difficult, and will take practice, is giving yourself permission to feel all that you are feeling and think all that you are thinking in the moment. In other words, the inner censor needs to be silenced. To help with this, morning pages are done on a pad of paper (not in a nice journal book), you do not correct spelling errors, and you do not read over what you have written. This exercise is about *process*, not product. Write whatever comes to mind; nothing is too petty, too silly, too stupid, or too weird to be included.

In order to release yourself into the Morning Pages, it is important that you know that nobody will read them except you. To be able to surrender fully into uncensored writing, you may need to speak to those close to you and ask them to destroy the pad of paper if something should happen to you. This may sound crazy, but you will find that your censor is very, very active, and the goal of Morning Pages is to truly give yourself the gift of receiving all of your thoughts and feelings in the moment. As you do so, they have the chance to change—witnessing is a powerful and freeing force.

You can read more about this process in *The Way of the Mysterial Woman*, chapter seven.

2. Create an altar and light a candle

The concept of having a space designated in your home for the sacred is shared across many cultures around the world. It is a way to honor and cultivate a connection with the invisible in a visible way.

When you are in the midst of chaos, confusion, and transition, your altar will become the outer symbol of beauty, order, and your intentions for the future. It becomes a home base or "true north" for you as you remember yourself and do the deep work of navigating through the territory of trauma and loss. As you spend time at your altar—first setting it up and then working with it on a daily basis—it will begin to bring you comfort and become a power place for you.

Decide what symbols you would like to add to your altar that would inspire you, support you, and help you to activate images of the future. Maybe it is a photo of your grandmother who always encouraged you, or maybe a stone or memento from a dear friend, or a statue of a spiritual icon that immediately takes you into a sense of the sacred. You do not want your altar to be cluttered, but you do want it to be alive with symbols of meaning to you. You may want to consider adding a bell or Tibetan bowl that you can ring on your way in and out of your sessions. Incense is another wonderful way to evoke your full sensory awareness and help you shift your state of being.

Include a candle on your altar as a way to initiate and close the times that you engage with it. For those who enjoy a scented candle, this is another great way to awaken your embodied sensibilities when you engage with your altar. A small vase of fresh flowers can provide not only a connection to beauty but also a useful way to ensure that you are tending and caring for this sacred space in an ongoing way. When it truly becomes an outer symbol of yourself, you will notice a correlation between the times when your altar gets dusty and the flowers are dead and the juiciness of your connection to yourself.

Once you have created your altar, take time each morning to light your candle and let the symbols and energy into your heart.

You can find out more about how to find the right place and create an altar in *The Way of the Mysterial Woman*, chapter five.

3. Read a poem for the day

Poetry was a vital component of my own healing, and I am deeply grateful for the guiding voices of the many poets, alive and dead, who held me, reassured me, reminded me, and inspired me along my path. A good poem engages both the seen and the unseen, feelings and thoughts, and speaks to where you are in a way that isn't as accessible through daily language. A good poem can also hold the vision of the future when your own eyes cannot see very far.

Choose a poem as a healing tincture for a period of time and take it deeply into yourself by printing it out, putting it on your phone, reading it daily, and perhaps even committing it to memory.

Please visit my website, MysterialWoman.com, for a list of the poems that held me tight during the darkest nights and were a guiding light on my path back home.

4. Meditation

Many of you reading this book will already be familiar with meditation and its value in helping us to become more mindful and present in the midst of our life circumstances. I have maintained a meditation practice for decades, and I've found it to be a critical daily practice. Following David's death, it became a place of stillness where I could watch my thoughts and feelings without attaching to them or needing to do anything about them. I could also feel the larger pattern that I was a part of—the deep field of loving awareness that was larger than "me" going through the struggles.

If you do not already have a meditation practice, there are many apps and websites that can help you to ease into one (some great ones are WakingUp.com, InsightTimer.com, Calm.com, and Headspace.com). You do not need to begin with long meditations; even ten minutes a day can make an enormous difference in your overall well-being.

5. Energize your intention out loud

In the earlier chapters of this book, you read about some of the ways I worked with holding a positive image of the future to call in the best possible path forward in my life—when trying to sell my home or find a new home, when opening to a partner, and in various rituals that I did. There is plenty of good research around that confirms that using the body, heart, and mind to magnetize a positive future possibility is an effective approach during times of chaos, and I have shared with you my lived personal experience of the potency of this process in this book. (See *The Way of the Mysterial Woman*, chapter fifteen, for more information).

To begin, do some stream-of-conscious writing around what kind of future you want to create. What does the phoenix arising from the ashes of your former life look and feel like? You do not need to know how you will get there.

Think/Feel/Sense into what is most important for you to experience now. Keep the following five elements in mind as you write your statement:

1. Write it in the positive (not the absence of something you don't like).
2. Write it in the present tense, as though it has already been accomplished.
3. Keep it short enough that you can call it to mind easily.
4. Begin with the words "I am . . ."

Once you have written the statement, say it aloud to yourself and see if it evokes positive and strong emotions in your body. See if each and every word resonates for you as you speak it aloud (you should feel something like a subtle vibration or lift of energy).

The potency of the Intention process has everything to do with the emotional energy your imagination has the power to activate in your body. Allow yourself to really feel this "future you" even though you have no idea how you will get there. Orient yourself toward a future possibility, a freedom that is embedded in a positive intention for yourself and the world.

Deep Practice for Turning Toward Your Feelings

In the midst of trauma and loss, there will of course be many feelings that will rise and fall like waves in an ocean. Learning to ride these waves instead of being pummeled by them or avoiding them is vitally important.

Take yourself through this short practice when you have been triggered into an emotional state that is overwhelming your system.

Observe: Cultivate the capacity of the observer, noticing when you are triggered into an intense emotional state. Ideally, you would take some time to journal on the following questions:

- What are the feelings and sensations in your body (tension, clenched stomach, sweaty palms, heart beating, fear, anxiety, anger)?
- What thoughts tend to accompany these feelings (*This isn't safe; I can't trust them; It wouldn't work anyway; Who do I think I am*)?
- When you are triggered like this, what is your conditioned behavioral response (fight, flight, freeze, fawn)? What behaviors are habitual and not very effective?

Allow: Allow the feelings to be there without pushing them away or exaggerating them. As much as possible, just be with the feeling wave and let it move through you.

Breathe: Let the mind be quiet (let all mental chatter go—worries from the past or stories about the future) and breathe into the feelings and sensations in the body. Go farther toward the feeling.

Investigate: Ask yourself what outdated limiting beliefs might be underneath this activation that feels like life and death. What do you believe from the past to be true? Is it still true? You can also check whether any of the five limiting beliefs our research uncovered as being present in the outdated unconscious inner operating system are active in you:

1. I am not enough
2. I have to do to be of value
3. I do not belong
4. I am not free to express myself fully
5. I don't have enough knowledge, connections, or influence

Center: As you begin to feel a release of the emotional feelings and sensations that have hijacked you, bring yourself to center. Find your ground by literally feeling your feet on the ground and taking in full, deep breaths from the center of your body. As you exhale, allow your muscles to relax into gravity and find yourself centered in three-dimensional space so that you become more fully present and your energy is balanced between the front and back, the right and left, and above and below.

Re-vision: Using your imagination take yourself back inside the experience that triggered you and re-vision a response that is sourced from this place of grounded presence. (Note: This step is a powerful way to open up new neural pathways for new behaviors. The brain does not distinguish between the lived experience and the visualization.)

Acknowledgments

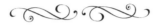

Living this journey was the first difficult task; gathering it up in a book was another one entirely. I simply could not have gotten through the trauma and loss and writing about it all without the rock-solid support, encouragement, and love of so many dear friends and family.

Thank you to Dianne Grob and Richard Chadek, who walked with me every day through all these years. Thank you for being my local family when I lost mine so suddenly: for our daily check-ins, Sunday dinners at your kitchen counter, important holidays together, and your unwavering belief that I could and should write this book. Thank you to the rest of my "trauma tribe" of dear friends who kept a loving circle around me for the first years: Sharleen Chesledon, Deborah Kennedy, Antonia Greene, Rob Synder, Sarah Keenan, Lynda Lowe, David Madeira, Rick Head, Julia Smith, Virginia Rhoads, John McConnell, Nota Lucas, Pattie Hanmer, David Pfeiffer, and Daniel Klein.

To my loving family, who took turns the first few month to be with me—dearest siblings Hannah, Peter, and Kathy Anderson; their deeply supportive spouses, Brian Bedard, Karen Anderson, and Kirk Mitchell; their children, especially Justin Bedard, Simon Bedard and his wife, Kelly Gray, and Cassandra Mitchell; and my cousin Sarah Schwartz—thank you all for steadying my capsized ship so that I could navigate into my new life.

Deepest gratitude to David's sister, Pam Avriett, who showed up for me again and again over the years in the midst of her own grief and profound loss. To her husband, Don Avriett, and to Claire Avriett Tirtoprodjo and Chris Tirtoprodjo and Peter Avriett, thank you for continuing to include me in your lives as family.

To my therapist and guide Erica Helm Meade, I thank you with all of my heart for walking with me every step of the way before, during, and after the tsunami of loss. Your wise and loving presence helped me to re-member myself, find my mythic thread, and share it with the world.

Thank you to Catherine Johnson and Susan Hormann, whose weekly healing sessions breathed life back into my exhausted body, heart, mind, and soul.

Thank you to Michael Meade who was there to usher me down into Hades and who guided many of the early rituals that brought some coherence to the shattered world left behind by David's chosen death. Thank you to Carol Lissance and Claudia Edwards who were deeply impacted and yet held steady in a commitment to loving friendship. To the myriad people who showed up in that first year—many of whom I never met—bringing food, creating videos, cleaning my house, hosting dinners, helping me sell paintings, and more, I deeply appreciated it all. The community was a resilience field of enormous support.

Thank you to Trish Maharam, who reached out her hand when I was taking the big leap from my life in Vashon to Seattle and made it possible for me to land in a healing sanctuary. I am deeply grateful for her generous heart and, along with Jennifer Wells and Sally Hulsman, the shared support for me to live in a beautiful home and office as I healed and made my way into the world again.

Thank you to Susan Cannon who kept our company going and tended to the women in the program that was meant to launch six days after David's death until we could run it five months later, and who worked with me to finally publish *The Way of the Mysterial Woman*. Thank you to my Mysterial faculty allies—Jamie Selby, Camille de Picot, Nota Lucas, and Astrid van den Broek in particular—who walked with me as I made my way back into the world of my global programs with women. Their belief in the work and commitment to it were powerful forces in my own journey. And thank you to the many women clients and students in my programs over the years who were often the reason that I kept on going with my work and with writing this book. It has been an honor to walk with them and learn from them as women on the edge of evolution.

To my editor Gail Hudson, who was instrumental in helping me—as she did with my first book, *The Way of the Mysterial Woman*, —to shape the raw materials of my journey into a coherent book, I am so deeply grateful. It was her guiding vision that convinced me my story could be a healing offering to others and resulted in this book.

Thank you to Lynda Lowe for allowing me to use her exquisite painting *Deeper Well* on my book cover. I was lucky enough to have Lynda's evocative painting *Boundless* on the cover of *The Way of the Mysterial Woman*, and it is powerfully symbolic to have the same exquisite vessel in both paintings on both covers.

And to my late husband David Smith, I stand now able to accept all the offerings that have come to me through his decision to leave this world. I remain infinitely grateful everyday for the ten years I spent together with him. He provided a deeply loving sanctuary within which I could become the person who could make her path by walking over the rugged landscape of loss. His loving and his leaving, and now my rebirth, have been the great transformational forces in my life.

My deepest gratitude to Richard Pleus, who met me as I began to emerge from the underworld of trauma and loss and, through his love, helped me to heal my broken heart and make my return to the upper world. His steadfast encouragement to tell my story and share it in this book was a constant wind at my back, and his loving partnership an enormous blessing in my life.

Finally, a deep bow to the darkness—the Yin field of the Great Mystery that broke me open to myself and to the world as I made my path by walking.

About the Author

Suzanne Anderson, MA, is the founder of The Mysterial Woman, a psychologist, author, coach, leadership consultant, and transformational teacher. Her pioneering work in guiding others to awaken their full Feminine and Masculine strengths combines insights and practices from ancient wisdom, depth psychology, and modern neuroscience. She has dedicated the past thirty years to decoding an embodied, integral, and accelerated archetypal pathway to unlock the next level of our innate potential. Combining her graduate studies in women's developmental psychology together with her decades as a leadership consultant, Suzanne wisely guides women to awaken to the next level of consciousness and leadership capacity, making the changes in themselves they want to shape in the world. She facilitates global online programs, workshops, and retreats, and is the coauthor of the triple award-winning book *The Way of the Mysterial Woman: Upgrading How You Live, Love, and Lead.* Originally from Canada, Suzanne now lives in Seattle, WA. To learn more about Suzanne and her work, please visit MysterialWoman.com.

Author photo © Mary Grace Long

SELECTED TITLES FROM SHE WRITES PRESS

She Writes Press is an independent publishing
company founded to serve women writers everywhere.
Visit us at www.shewritespress.com.

The Way of the Mysterial Woman: Upgrading How You Live, Love, and Lead by Suzanne Anderson, MA and Susan Cannon, PhD. $24.95, 978-1-63152-081-5. A revolutionary yet practical road map for upgrading your life, work, and relationships that reveals how your choice to transform is part of an astonishing future trend.

The World Looks Different Now: A Memoir of Suicide, Faith, and Family by Margaret Thomson. $16.95, 978-1-63152-693-0. The gripping, intensely personal story of a mother struggling to come to terms with the suicide of her twenty-two-year-old son only weeks before he was due to deploy to Afghanistan.

The First Signs of April: A Memoir by Mary-Elizabeth Briscoe. $16.95, 978-1-63152-298-7. Briscoe explores the destructive patterns of unresolved grief and the importance of connection for true healing to occur in this inspirational memoir, which weaves through time to explore grief reactions to two very different losses: suicide and cancer.

Sandwiched: A Memoir of Holding on and Letting Go by Laurie James. $16.95, 978-1-63152-785-2. After her mother has a heart attack and her husband's lawyer delivers some shocking news, James finds herself sandwiched between caring for her parents, managing caregivers, raising four daughters, and trying to understand her husband's choices—so, to keep herself afloat, she seeks therapy, practices yoga, rediscovers nature, and begins to write. Will it be enough to keep her family together?

The Art of Losing it: A Memoir of Grief and Addiction by Rosemary Keevil. $16.95, 978-1-63152-777-7. When her husband dies of cancer and her brother dies of AIDS in the same year, Rosemary is left to raise her two young daughters on her own and plunged into a hurricane of grief—a hurricane from which she seeks refuge in drugs and alcohol.

The Buddha at My Table: How I Found Peace in Betrayal and Divorce by Tammy Letherer. $16.95, 978-1-63152-425-7. On a Tuesday night, just before Christmas, after he had put their three children in bed, Tammy Letherer's husband shattered her world and destroyed every assumption she'd ever made about love, friendship, and faithfulness. In the aftermath of this betrayal, however, she finds unexpected blessings—and, ultimately, the path to freedom.